Betty Crocker

just
cupcakes

100 Recipes for the Way You Really Cook

WILEY

Wiley Publishing, Inc

Library of Congress Cataloging-in-Publication Data:

Crocker, Betty.
  Betty Crocker just cupcakes : 100 recipes for the way you really cook.
    p. cm.
  Includes index.
  ISBN 978-0-470-32729-6 (cloth/spiral-bound : alk. paper)
  1. Cupcakes. I. Title. II. Title: Just cupcakes.
  TX771.C6994 2008
  641.8'653--dc22
                        2008009427

General Mills
Betty Crocker Kitchens:

Publisher, Cookbooks: Maggie Gilbert/Lynn Vettel

Manager and Editor, Cookbooks: Lois Tlusty

Food Editor: Andi Bidwell

Recipe Development and Testing: Betty Crocker Kitchens

Photography: General Mills Photography Studios and Image Library

Printed in China
10 9 8 7 6 5 4 3 2

Cover photo: Anniversary White Truffle Cupcakes (page 82)

Wiley Publishing, Inc.:

Publisher: Natalie Chapman

Executive Editor: Anne Ficklen

Editor: Adam Kowit

Production Manager: Michael Olivo

Cover Design: Suzanne Sunwoo

Interior Design: Tai Blanche

Layout: Indianapolis Composition Services

Manufacturing Manager: Kevin Watt

Our Betty Crocker Kitchens seal guarantees success in your kitchen. Every recipe has been tested in America's Most Trusted Kitchens™ to meet our high standards of reliability, easy preparation and great taste.

Find more great ideas at *BettyCrocker.com*

Dear Friends,

A cupcake is one of life's simple pleasures. What could be better than a batch of homemade cupcakes (or two!) decorated to suit any occasion? Here you'll find recipes from everyday to elegant, from frosted to filled, from absolutely adorable to fabulously fun.

Decorating is so easy that it's a great way to get the kids involved. Let the littlest ones poke the polka dots into the frosting of the Spring Polka Dot Cupcakes. Older kids can build the marshmallow ghosts for the Ghost Cupcakes or "draw" the soccer balls on the Ball Game Cupcakes.

Or get everyone involved in a cupcake family portrait. Set out your favorite frosted cupcakes and decorations, and let everyone decorate a cupcake to look like someone else in the family—don't forget the goldfish and the dog!

Inspired by all the possibilities and have your own ideas? Turn to the basics chapter for all the cake and frosting recipes you need to create your own cupcake sensations!

So grab your muffin pan, make new memories and cherish the smiles.

Enjoy!
Betty Crocker

contents

Cupcakes, Short and Sweet

What's great about cupcakes is that a few basic skills, tools and ingredients are all you need to make cupcakes for any occasion, whether they're for a party that's a month away or you're in the mood for a spur-of-the-moment batch.

Cupcake Baker's Pantry

With these basic items always on hand, you can make and decorate a batch of cupcakes whenever you like. For many recipes, your grocery list of ingredients will be a short one.

EQUIPMENT:

- Muffin pans (mini and regular), available in metal or silicone.

- Paper baking cups (mini and regular), available in a variety of colors and themed and seasonal prints. Look for them in your supermarket, party store, craft store or specialty cake decorating store.

- Small resealable food-storage plastic bags for piping icings and glazes.

PANTRY STAPLES:

The decorations are available at your supermarket in the baking section.

- Boxed cake mixes. Yellow, white and devil's food cake mixes with pudding in the mix are good to have on hand.

- Ready-to-spread frostings. Creamy chocolate, vanilla and white frostings are good staples.

- Decorating icing in assorted colors.

- Decorating gels in assorted colors.

- Food colors (liquid, gel or paste). Try paste food color; the color is more concentrated, so a little goes a long way.

- Assorted colored sugars and edible glitters.

- Assorted candy sprinkles, available in a variety of colors and shapes.

Muffin Pans

A typical cupcake recipe makes 24 cupcakes in regular-size muffin cups. Muffin pans with regular-size cups come in 6-muffin or 12-muffin sizes. There are also pans that have mini, large and jumbo muffin cups. Mini muffin pans make 24 cupcakes, large and jumbo muffin pans make 6 cupcakes each.

PAN TYPE	CUP SIZE
Mini	1¾ x 1 inches
Regular	2½ x 1¼ inches
Large	2¾ x 1¼ inches
Jumbo	3½ x 1¾ inches

If you have only one muffin pan and a recipe calls for more cupcakes than your pan will make, just cover and refrigerate the rest of the batter while baking the first batch. Cool the pan about 15 minutes, then bake the rest of the batter, adding 1 to 2 minutes to the bake time.

An easy way to fill muffin cups is to use an ice cream scoop. Use one that measures out ⅓ cup batter when filling regular-size muffin cups. Use one that measures out 2 tablespoons batter when filling mini muffin cups.

Time-Saving Tips

An easy way to frost cupcakes is to carefully dip tops into the frosting, give a slight twist and remove. Finish off with a swirl of a knife if needed. You can also use this dipping method to add toppings to frosted cupcakes.

To decorate frosted cupcakes quickly, place nuts, colored sugar, sprinkles, or other decors into small bowls and lightly tap the frosted cupcake upside down into the topping to coat as desired.

Create Your Own Designs

For an alternative to frosting your cupcakes, you can glaze or dust; here's how:

- Glaze: Choose a glaze recipe (pages 152–153). Evenly spread or drizzle in an interesting design on top of cooled cupcakes. To make drizzling easier, pour glaze into a heavy-duty food-storage plastic bag, snip off a tiny corner of the bag and squeeze. Check out Cherry Mini Cakes (page 79) and Stars and Stripes Cupcakes (page 96).

- Dust: Simply dust lightly or as desired through a shaker, sieve or sifter. For a more dramatic look, place a doily, stencil or simple cutout shape on the cupcake before dusting then carefully remove the pattern. Check out the Heart Brownie Cupcakes (page 88).

Create a new look with these decorating ideas. If you don't find them at your supermarket, try a cake decorating store.

- Pearl Sugar: White sugar grains add interest to cupcakes for special occasions like showers and weddings.

- Crystal and Sanding Sugar: Sprinkle this glistening, colorful sugar on frosted cakes and cupcakes.

- Food Writer Pens: Use as you would ink markers to add dazzling color.

- Decorating Spray: Spray on cupcakes; it dries to form a powdery coating. The look is similar to a technique used by bakeries.

A cupcake doesn't have to be just a cupcake! Use your imagination and cut cupcakes to look like something else. Check out Baby Bootie Shower Cakes (page 78) and Baseball Caps (page 121). You can also arrange them together to make something larger. Check out Pull-Apart Turtle Cupcakes (page 130).

Storing Unfrosted and Frosted Cupcakes

To keep your baked cupcakes fresh:

- Cool cupcakes completely before covering and storing to keep the tops from becoming sticky.

- Cover cupcakes that will be frosted later loosely so the tops stay dry. If covered tightly, they become sticky and difficult to frost.

- Store cupcakes with a creamy-type frosting loosely covered with foil, plastic wrap or waxed paper or under a cake safe or inverted bowl.

- Refrigerate cupcakes with whipped cream toppings or cream fillings.

- Frost cupcakes with fluffy frosting on the day they're to be served.

Freezing Cupcakes

Get a head start; bake cupcakes ahead of time and freeze until you need them. Unfrosted cupcakes freeze better than frosted. Frozen cupcakes are also easier to frost! When freezing unfrosted cupcakes:

- Cool unfrosted cupcakes completely, about 30 minutes, before covering and storing to keep the tops from becoming sticky.

- Place cupcakes in cardboard bakery boxes to prevent crushing, then tightly cover with foil, plastic wrap or larger freezer bags. Properly packaged, unfrosted cakes can be kept frozen two to three months.

Creamy-type frostings freeze best. Fluffy-type and whipped cream frostings freeze well but may stick to the wrapping.

- To prevent frosting from sticking, freeze cupcakes uncovered 1 hour, then insert a toothpick in the top of the cupcake, and tightly wrap. Frozen frosted cupcakes keep two to three months.

- Thaw cupcakes in the refrigerator or on the countertop. When thawing on the countertop, loosen or remove wrapping to prevent condensation from forming.

Decorating gel, hard candies and colored sugars do not freeze well because they tend to run during thawing.

1

everyday treats

Super-Easy Cupcakes

Prep Time: 15 min ▪ Start to Finish: 1 hr ▪ 24 cupcakes

3 cups Original Bisquick® mix
1 cup sugar
1/4 cup shortening
1 cup milk or water
2 teaspoons vanilla
2 eggs
1 container (1 lb) creamy ready-to-spread frosting (any flavor)

1 Heat oven to 375°F. Grease and flour 24 regular-size muffin cups, or line with foil or paper baking cups.

2 In large bowl, beat all ingredients except frosting with electric mixer on low speed 30 seconds, scraping bowl constantly. Beat on medium speed 4 minutes, scraping bowl occasionally. Divide batter evenly among muffin cups.

3 Bake about 15 minutes or until toothpick inserted in center of cupcake comes out clean. Immediately remove from pan to cooling rack. Cool completely, about 1 hour. Frost cupcakes. Decorate if desired.

1 Cupcake: Calories 125 (Calories from Fat 45); Total Fat 5g (Saturated Fat 1g); Cholesterol 20mg; Sodium 220mg; Total Carbohydrate 18g (Dietary Fiber 0g)

Kids love cupcakes! To make decorating these kid-friendly treats even easier, freeze the unfrosted baked cupcakes for up to three months. Frozen cupcakes are easier to frost, and you can decorate them any way you like.

Tie-Dyed Cupcakes

Prep Time: 15 min ▪ Start to Finish: 1 hr 25 min ▪ 24 Cupcakes

1 box (1 lb 2.25 oz) white or yellow cake mix with pudding in the mix
Water, vegetable oil and egg whites called for on cake mix box
1 container (9 oz) multicolored candy sprinkles

1 Heat oven to 350°F. Place paper baking cups in each of 24 regular-size muffin cups. Make cake as directed on box for 24 cupcakes using water, oil and egg whites, except fill muffin cups half full; top each with ¼ teaspoon sprinkles. Top with remaining batter; sprinkle each with ½ teaspoon sprinkles.

2 Bake and cool as directed on box for cupcakes.

1 Cupcake: Calories 170 (Calories from Fat 60); Total Fat 7g (Saturated Fat 2.5g); Cholesterol 0mg; Sodium 160mg; Total Carbohydrate 25g (Dietary Fiber 0g)

Easy Design Cupcakes

Prep Time: 40 min ▪ Start to Finish: 1 hr 50 min ▪ 24 Cupcakes

2 packages (3 oz each) cream cheese, softened
1/3 cup sugar
1 egg
1 bag (6 oz) semisweet chocolate chips (1 cup)
1 box (1 lb 2.25 oz) devil's food cake mix with pudding in the mix
Water, vegetable oil and eggs called for on cake mix box
1 1/2 oz cream cheese (from 3-oz package), softened
4 teaspoons sugar

1 Heat oven to 350°F. Place paper baking cup in each of 24 regular-size muffin cups. In medium bowl, beat 2 packages cream cheese, 1/3 cup sugar and the egg with electric mixer on medium speed until smooth. Stir in chocolate chips; set aside.

2 Make cake mix as directed on box, using water, oil and eggs. Divide batter evenly among muffin cups. Top each with 1 tablespoon cream cheese mixture (mixture will sink into batter).

3 In small bowl, beat 1½ ounces cream cheese and 4 teaspoons sugar with spoon until smooth. Spoon into corner of small plastic food-storage bag. Cut ⅛ inch tip off 1 bottom corner of bag. Pipe mixture onto batter in a small design to decorate tops of cupcakes.

4 Bake 20 to 25 minutes or until tops spring back when touched lightly. Cool 10 minutes; remove from pan to cooling rack. Cool completely, about 50 minutes.

1 Cupcake (Cake and Frosting): Calories 220 (Calories from Fat 110); Total Fat 12g (Saturated Fat 5g); Cholesterol 45mg; Sodium 200mg; Total Carbohydrate 26g (Dietary Fiber 1g)

Chocolate Chip Cheesecake Swirl Cupcakes

Prep Time: 30 min ▪ Start to Finish: 1 hr 5 min ▪ 24 Cupcakes

1/2 cup sugar
2 packages (3 oz each) cream cheese, softened
1 egg
1 bag (6 oz) semisweet chocolate chips (1 cup)
2 1/4 cups all-purpose flour
1 2/3 cups sugar
1/4 cup unsweetened baking cocoa
1 1/4 cups water
1/2 cup vegetable oil
2 tablespoons white vinegar
2 teaspoons baking soda
2 teaspoons vanilla
1 teaspoon salt

1 Heat oven to 350°F. Place paper baking cups in each of 24 regular-size muffin cups. In medium bowl, beat ½ cup sugar and the cream cheese with electric mixer on medium speed until smooth. Beat in egg. Stir in chocolate chips; set aside.

2 In large bowl, beat remaining ingredients on low speed 30 seconds, scraping bowl occasionally. Beat on high speed 3 minutes, scraping bowl occasionally. Reserve 1½ cups batter.

3 Fill each muffin cup one-third full (1 round tablespoon). Spoon 1 tablespoon cream cheese mixture onto batter in each cup. Top each with reserved batter (½ rounded tablespoon).

4 Bake 30 to 35 minutes or until toothpick inserted in center comes out clean.

1 Cupcake: Calories 220 (Calories from Fat 90); Total Fat 10g (Saturated Fat 3.5g); Cholesterol 15mg; Sodium 230mg; Total Carbohydrate 32g (Dietary Fiber 1g)

Sour Cream Chocolate Cupcakes

Prep Time: 30 min ▪ Start to Finish: 55 min ▪ 36 Cupcakes

Cupcakes
2 cups all-purpose flour
2 cups granulated sugar
3/4 cup sour cream
1/4 cup shortening
1 cup water
1 1/4 teaspoons baking soda
1 teaspoon salt
1 teaspoon vanilla
1/2 teaspoon baking powder
2 eggs
4 oz unsweetened baking
    chocolate, melted and cooled

Rich Chocolate Buttercream Frosting
4 cups powdered sugar
1 cup butter or margarine, softened
3 tablespoons milk
1 1/2 teaspoons vanilla
3 oz unsweetened baking
    chocolate, melted and cooled

1 Heat oven to 350°F. Place paper baking cup in each of 36 regular-size muffin cups. In large bowl, beat all cupcake ingredients with electric mixer on low speed 30 seconds, scraping bowl constantly. Beat on high speed 3 minutes, scraping bowl occasionally. Divide batter evenly among muffin cups.

2 Bake 20 to 25 minutes or until toothpick inserted in center comes out clean. Remove from pan; place on cooling rack. Cool completely.

3 In medium bowl, beat all frosting ingredients with electric mixer on medium speed until smooth and spreadable. If necessary, stir in additional milk, 1 teaspoon at a time. Frost cupcakes.

1 Cupcake: Calories 240 (Calories from Fat 100); Total Fat 11g (Saturated Fat 6g); Cholesterol 30mg; Sodium 160mg; Total Carbohydrate 32g (Dietary Fiber 1g)

Use ready-to-spread chocolate frosting instead of the home-made buttercream. You'll still get rave reviews for these sensational sweets!

Red Velvet Cupcakes with Cream Cheese Frosting

Prep Time: 20 min ▪ Start to Finish: 2 hr ▪ 24 Cupcakes

1 teaspoon water
1 bottle (1 oz) red food color
1 box (1 lb 2.25 oz) devil's food cake
  mix with pudding in the mix

Water, vegetable oil and eggs called
  for on cake mix box
1 container (1 lb) cream cheese
  creamy ready-to-spread frosting

1 Heat oven to 375°F. Place paper baking cup in each of 24 regular-size muffin cups. In small bowl, mix 1 teaspoon water and 3 or 4 drops of the food color; set aside.

2 In large bowl, beat cake mix, 1¼ cups water, the oil, eggs and remaining bottle of food color with electric mixer on low speed 30 seconds. Beat on medium speed 2 minutes, scraping bowl occasionally. Divide batter evenly among muffin cups.

3 Bake 18 to 23 minutes or until toothpick inserted in center comes out clean. Cool 10 minutes; remove from pan to cooling rack. Cool completely, about 30 minutes.

4 Frost cupcakes. Using a fine-tip brush, paint cupcakes with red food color paint, swirling paint to create design. Store loosely covered at room temperature.

1 Cupcake: Calories 220 (Calories from Fat 100); Total Fat 11g (Saturated Fat 3g); Cholesterol 25mg; Sodium 220mg; Total Carbohydrate 29g (Dietary Fiber 0g)

Jazz up these cupcakes by serving with vanilla ice cream topped with red candy sprinkles or a drizzle of grenadine syrup.

Banana Toffee Cupcakes

Prep Time: 15 min ▪ Start to Finish: 40 min ▪ 36 Cupcakes

1 box (1 lb 2.25 oz) golden vanilla cake mix with pudding in the mix
1/3 cup water
1/2 cup vegetable oil
3 eggs
1 teaspoon almond extract
3 medium bananas, mashed (1¼ cups)
1 package (6 oz) toffee chips (1 cup)

1 Heat oven to 350°F. Place paper baking cup in each of 36 regular-size muffin cups.

2 In large bowl, beat cake mix, water, oil, eggs and almond extract with electric mixer on low speed 30 seconds. Beat on medium speed 2 minutes. Beat in bananas until smooth. Stir in toffee chips. Divide batter evenly among muffin cups.

3 Bake about 25 minutes or until golden brown; immediately remove from pan.

1 Cupcake: Calories 125 (Calories from Fat 55); Total Fat 6g (Saturated Fat 2g); Cholesterol 25mg; Sodium 105mg; Total Carbohydrate 17g (Dietary Fiber 0g)

Stir in 1 cup miniature semisweet chocolate chips in place of the toffee chips, or for the really indulgent, toss in a cup of both!

Candy-Sprinkled Cupcakes

Prep Time: 20 min ▪ Start to Finish: 1 hr 30 min ▪ 24 Cupcakes

1 box (1 lb 2.25 oz) yellow or white cake mix with pudding in the mix
Water, vegetable oil and eggs called for on cake mix box
1 container (12 oz) fluffy white whipped ready-to-spread frosting
Pastel candy sprinkles

1 Heat oven to 350°F. Make and bake cake as directed on box for 24 cupcakes, using water, oil and eggs. Cool in pan 10 minutes; remove from pan to cooling rack. Cool completely, about 30 minutes.

2 Frost cupcakes with frosting.

3 To decorate, roll edge of each cupcake in candy sprinkles. Store loosely covered.

1 Cupcake (Cake and Frosting): Calories 190 (Calories from Fat 80); Total Fat 8g (Saturated Fat 2.5g); Cholesterol 25mg; Sodium 160mg; Total Carbohydrate 26g (Dietary Fiber 0g)

Strawberry and Cream Cupcakes

Prep Time: 30 min ▮ Start to Finish: 1 hr 30 min ▮ 24 Cupcakes

> 1 box (1 lb 2.25 oz) white cake mix with pudding in the mix
> 1¼ cups strawberry carbonated beverage
> Vegetable oil and egg whites called for on cake mix box
> Red food color
> 1 container (1 lb) cream cheese creamy ready-to-spread frosting
> ½ cup white candy sprinkles
> Fresh strawberries, if desired

1 Heat oven to 350°F. Place paper baking cups in each of 24 regular-size muffin cups. Make and bake cake mix as directed on box for 24 cupcakes, substituting carbonated beverage for the water and using oil and egg whites. Cool 10 minutes; remove from pan to cooling rack. Cool completely, about 30 minutes.

2 Stir 1 or 2 drops food color into frosting. Frost cupcakes.

3 In small resealable food-storage plastic bag, place sprinkles and 1 drop food color; seal bag. Gently shake and massage decors until mixture is various shades of pink; sprinkle around edges of frosted cupcakes. Garnish with fresh strawberries.

1 Cupcake: Calories 230 (Calories from Fat 90); Total Fat 10g (Saturated Fat 3g); Cholesterol 0mg; Sodium 200mg; Total Carbohydrate 32g (Dietary Fiber 0g)

Toasted Almond Cupcakes with Caramel Frosting

Prep Time: 25 min ▌ Start to Finish: 2 hr 5 min ▌ 24 Cupcakes

Cupcakes

1/2 cup slivered almonds

1 box (1 lb 2.25 oz) white cake mix
   with pudding in the mix

11/4 cups water

1/3 cup vegetable oil

3 eggs

1 teaspoon almond extract

1 cup sliced almonds

Caramel Frosting

1/2 cup butter or margarine

1 cup packed brown sugar

1/4 cup milk

2 cups powdered sugar

1 Heat oven to 375°F. Place paper baking cup in each of 24 regular-size muffin cups. In shallow pan, bake slivered almonds 6 to 10 minutes, stirring occasionally, until golden brown; cool 15 minutes. In food processor, grind the toasted almonds until finely ground.

2 In large bowl, beat cake mix, water, oil, eggs and almond extract with electric mixer on low speed 30 seconds. Beat on medium speed 2 minutes, scraping bowl occasionally. Fold in ground almonds.

3 Divide batter among muffin cups. Bake 20 to 24 minutes or until toothpick inserted in center comes out clean. Cool 10 minutes. Remove from pan to cooling rack. Cool completely. Meanwhile, in shallow pan, bake sliced almonds at 375°F for 5 to 8 minutes, stirring occasionally, until golden brown.

4 In 2-quart saucepan, melt butter over medium heat. Stir in brown sugar. Heat to boiling, stirring constantly; reduce heat to low. Boil and stir 2 minutes. Stir in milk. Heat to boiling; remove from heat. Cool to lukewarm, about 30 minutes.

5 Gradually stir powdered sugar into brown sugar mixture. Place saucepan in bowl of cold water. Beat with spoon until smooth and spreadable. If frosting becomes too stiff, stir in additional milk, 1 teaspoon at a time. Frost a few cupcakes at a time; press sliced almonds lightly into frosting.

1 Cupcake: Calories 280 (Calories from Fat 120); Total Fat 13g (Saturated Fat 3.5g); Cholesterol 35mg; Sodium 180mg; Total Carbohydrate 37g (Dietary Fiber 1g)

Satisfy a serious caramel craving by using real butter and dark brown sugar.

Peanut Butter Cupcakes with Chocolate Frosting

Prep Time: 40 min ▪ Start to Finish: 1 hr 35 min ▪ 30 Cupcakes

1 box (1 lb 2.25 oz) yellow cake mix with pudding in the mix
Water, vegetable oil and eggs called for on cake mix box
³/₄ cup creamy peanut butter
1 container (1 lb) chocolate creamy ready-to-spread frosting
¹/₄ cup creamy peanut butter
¹/₃ cup chopped peanuts

1 Heat oven to 350°F. Place paper baking cup in each of 30 regular-size muffin cups. In large bowl, beat cake mix, water, oil, eggs and ¾ cup peanut butter with electric mixer on low speed 30 seconds. Beat on medium speed 2 minutes, scraping bowl occasionally. Divide batter evenly among muffin cups.

2 Bake 20 to 25 minutes or until toothpick inserted in center comes out clean. Cool 10 minutes; remove from pan to cooling rack. Cool completely, about 30 minutes.

3 In medium bowl, stir together frosting and ¼ cup peanut butter. Frost cupcakes with frosting mixture. Sprinkle with peanuts; press lightly into frosting.

1 Cupcake: Calories 280 (Calories from Fat 140); Total Fat 15g (Saturated Fat 3.5g); Cholesterol 25mg; Sodium 270mg; Total Carbohydrate 30g (Dietary Fiber 0g)

Want to add more chocolate? Sprinkle the cupcakes with candy-coated peanut butter candies instead of the peanuts.

Brownie Cupcakes with Peanut Butter Frosting

Prep Time: 30 min ▮ Start to Finish: 1 hr ▮ 12 Cupcakes

Brownie Cupcakes
1 box (1 lb 6.5 oz) supreme brownie
   mix with pouch of chocolate
   flavor syrup
$1/3$ cup water
$1/3$ cup vegetable oil
2 or 3 eggs
Candy sprinkles, nonpareils or
   colored sugars, if desired

Peanut Butter Frosting and Garnish
1 cup vanilla creamy ready-to-
   spread frosting (from 1-lb
   container)
$1/3$ cup peanut butter
2 to 3 teaspoons milk
Candy sprinkles, if desired

1 Heat oven to 350°F. Place paper baking cup in each of 12 regular-size muffin cups, or grease bottoms only of muffin cups. In medium bowl, stir brownie mix, chocolate syrup, water, oil and 2 eggs for fudgelike brownies (or 3 eggs for cakelike brownies), using spoon, until well blended. Divide batter evenly among muffin cups.

2 Bake 28 to 30 minutes or until toothpick inserted in center comes out clean or almost clean. Cool 5 minutes; remove from pan to cooling rack. Cool completely.

3 In small bowl, mix all frosting ingredients until smooth and spreadable. Frost brownies; sprinkle with candy sprinkles. Store tightly covered.

1 Cupcake: Calories 640 (Calories from Fat 305); Total Fat 34g (Saturated Fat 12g); Cholesterol 75mg; Sodium 60mg; Total Carbohydrate 79g (Dietary Fiber 3g)

Mini Candy Bar Cupcakes

Prep Time: 20 min ▮ Start to Finish: 1 hr 5 min ▮ 72 Mini cupcakes

5 bars (2.1 oz each) chocolate-covered crispy peanut-buttery candy
1 box (1 lb 2.25 oz) white cake mix with pudding in the mix
Water, vegetable oil and egg whites called for on cake mix box
1 container (12 oz) milk chocolate whipped ready-to-spread frosting

1 Heat oven to 350°F. Place paper baking cup in each of 72 mini muffin cups. Finely chop enough candy to equal ¾ cup (about 1½ bars); set aside.

2 Make cake mix as directed on package, using water, oil and egg whites. Beat in chopped candy on low speed just until blended. Divide batter evenly among muffin cups. Refrigerate any remaining cake batter until ready to use.

3 Bake 13 to 15 minutes or until cupcakes spring back when touched lightly in center. Remove from pan to cooling rack. Cool completely, about 30 minutes. Frost cupcakes with frosting. Coarsely chop remaining candy. Place candy pieces on frosting, pressing down slightly. Store cupcakes loosely covered at room temperature.

1 Mini cupcake: Calories 80 (Calories from Fat 35); Total Fat 3.5g (Saturated Fat 1.5g); Cholesterol 0mg; Sodium 65mg; Total Carbohydrate 11g (Dietary Fiber 0g)

Malted Milk Ball Cupcakes

Prep Time: 20 min ▪ Start to Finish: 1 hr 25 min ▪ 24 Cupcakes

Cupcakes

1 box (1 lb 2.25 oz) yellow cake mix
  with pudding in the mix
1 cup malted milk balls, coarsely
  crushed
1/4 cup natural-flavor malted milk
  powder
1 1/4 cups water
1/3 cup vegetable oil
3 eggs

Frosting and Garnish

1/4 cup butter or margarine, softened
2 cups powdered sugar
2 tablespoons natural-flavor
  malted milk powder
1 tablespoon unsweetened baking
  cocoa
2 tablespoons milk
1 2/3 cups malted milk balls, coarsely
  crushed

1 Heat oven to 350°F. Place paper baking cup in each of 24 regular-size muffin cups. In large bowl, mix cake mix, 1 cup malted milk balls and 1/4 cup malted milk powder. Add water, oil and eggs. Beat with electric mixer on low speed 2 minutes. Divide batter evenly among muffin cups.

2 Bake 18 to 23 minutes or until toothpick inserted in center comes out clean. Cool 10 minutes; remove from pan to cooling rack. Cool completely, about 30 minutes.

3 In medium bowl, beat all frosting ingredients except malted milk balls on medium speed until smooth. Frost cupcakes. Sprinkle with 1 2/3 cups malted milk balls.

1 Cupcake: Calories 240 (Calories from Fat 90); Total Fat 10g (Saturated Fat 4.5g); Cholesterol 30mg; Sodium 190mg; Total Carbohydrate 37g (Dietary Fiber 0g)

Double-Coconut Cupcakes

Prep Time: 35 min ▮ Start to Finish: 1 hr 45 min ▮ 24 Cupcakes

2 cups flaked coconut
1/2 cup sweetened condensed milk (from 14-oz can; not evaporated)
1 box (1 lb 2.25 oz) yellow cake mix with pudding in the mix
Water, vegetable oil and eggs called for on cake mix box
Coconut Cream Frosting (page 147) or 1 container (1 lb) vanilla creamy
    ready-to-spread frosting
1 cup flaked coconut, toasted*

1 Heat oven to 375°F. Place paper baking cup in each of 24 regular-size muffin cups. In medium bowl, stir 2 cups coconut and the condensed milk; set aside.

2 In large bowl, beat cake mix, water, oil and eggs with electric mixer on low speed 30 seconds. Beat on medium speed 2 minutes, scraping bowl occasionally. Divide batter evenly among muffin cups. Top each with about 1 heaping teaspoonful coconut mixture.

3 Bake 15 to 22 minutes or until top springs back when lightly touched. Cool 5 minutes; remove from pan to cooling rack. Cool completely, about 30 minutes.

4 Make Coconut Cream Frosting; immediately frost cupcakes. Dip tops of cupcakes in toasted coconut. Store loosely covered at room temperature.

1 Cupcake: Calories 280 (Calories from Fat 110); Total Fat 12g (Saturated Fat 6g); Cholesterol 35mg; Sodium 220mg; Total Carbohydrate 40g (Dietary Fiber 0g)

*To toast the coconut, bake in a shallow pan at 350°F for 5 to 7 minutes, stirring occasionally, until golden brown.

Marshmallow Creme–Filled Cupcakes

Prep Time: 30 min ▪ Start to Finish: 1 hr 20 min ▪ 24 Cupcakes

Cupcakes
1 box (1 lb 2.25 oz) devil's food cake
    mix with pudding in the mix
Water, vegetable oil and eggs
    called for on cake mix box

Filling
1 cup vanilla whipped ready-to-
    spread frosting (from 12-oz
    container)

$^{1}/_{2}$ cup marshmallow creme

Frosting
1 cup chocolate whipped ready-
    to-spread frosting (from 12-oz
    container)
$^{1}/_{2}$ cup semisweet chocolate chips
2 teaspoons corn syrup
3 tablespoons vanilla whipped
    ready-to-spread frosting

1 Heat oven to 350°F. Place paper baking cup in each of 24 regular-size muffin cups. Make and bake cake mix as directed on box for 24 cupcakes, using water, oil and eggs. Cool 10 minutes; remove from pan to cooling rack. Cool completely, about 30 minutes.

2 With the end of round handle of wooden spoon or a melon baller, make deep, ½-inch-wide indentation in center of each cupcake, not quite to the bottom (wiggle end of spoon in cupcake to make opening large enough). In small bowl, mix 1 cup vanilla frosting and the marshmallow creme. Spoon into small resealable food-storage plastic bag. Cut ⅜-inch tip off 1 bottom corner of bag. Insert tip of bag into each cupcake and squeeze bag to fill.

3 In small microwavable bowl, microwave chocolate frosting, chocolate chips and corn syrup uncovered on High 30 seconds; stir. Microwave 15 to 30 seconds longer; stir until smooth. Dip top of each cupcake in frosting. Let stand until frosting is set.

4 Spoon 3 tablespoons vanilla frosting into small resealable food-storage plastic bag. Cut tiny tip off 1 bottom corner of bag. Pipe a squiggle of frosting or initials across top of each cupcake.

1 Cupcake: Calories 240 (Calories from Fat 100); Total Fat 11g (Saturated Fat 3.5g); Cholesterol 25mg; Sodium 210mg; Total Carbohydrate 32g (Dietary Fiber 1g)

Lemon-Filled Cupcakes

Prep Time: 25 min ▪ Start to Finish: 3 hr 25 min ▪ 30 Cupcakes

Lemon Filling (page 153)	3$^1/_2$ teaspoons baking powder
2$^1/_4$ cups all-purpose flour	1 teaspoon salt
1$^2/_3$ cups sugar	1 teaspoon vanilla
$^2/_3$ cup shortening	5 egg whites
1$^1/_4$ cups milk	White Mountain Frosting (page 150)

1 Make Lemon Filling. Heat oven to 350°F. Place paper baking cup in each of 30 regular-size muffin cups.

2 In large bowl, beat flour, sugar, shortening, milk, baking powder, salt and vanilla with electric mixer on low speed 30 seconds, scraping bowl constantly. Beat on high speed 2 minutes, scraping bowl occasionally. Beat in egg whites on high speed 2 minutes, scraping bowl occasionally. Divide batter evenly among muffin cups.

3 Bake 20 to 25 minutes, or until tops spring back when touched lightly. Cool 10 minutes; remove from pan to cooling rack. Cool completely, about 30 minutes.

4 Spoon filling into resealable heavy-duty food-storage plastic bag. Cut about ¼ inch tip off 1 bottom corner of bag. Gently push cut corner of bag into center of cupcake. Squeeze about 2 teaspoons filling into center of each cupcake, being careful not to split cupcake.

5 Make White Mountain Frosting. Frost cupcakes. Store cupcakes covered in the refrigerator.

1 Cupcake: Calories 410 (Calories from Fat 120); Total Fat 13g (Saturated Fat 3.5g); Cholesterol 0mg; Sodium 450mg; Total Carbohydrate 67g (Dietary Fiber 0g)

Molten Chocolate Cupcakes

Prep Time: 30 min ▪ Start to Finish: 2 hr ▪ 18 Cupcakes

$^1/_2$ cup whipping cream

1 cup semisweet chocolate chips (6 oz)

1 box (1 lb 2.25 oz) devil's food cake mix with pudding in the mix

Water, vegetable oil and eggs called for on cake mix box

1 container (1 lb) chocolate creamy ready-to-spread frosting

Powdered sugar, if desired

Sliced strawberries, if desired

1 In 1-quart saucepan, heat whipping cream over medium-high heat until hot but not boiling. Stir in chocolate chips until melted and mixture is smooth. Refrigerate about 1 hour, stirring occasionally, until thick.

2 Heat oven to 350°F. Spray 18 large muffin cups with baking spray with flour. In large bowl, beat cake mix, water, oil and eggs with electric mixer on low speed 30 seconds; beat on medium speed 2 minutes, scraping bowl constantly. Divide batter evening among muffin cups. Spoon 1 tablespoon cold chocolate mixture on top of batter in center of each cup.

3 Bake 18 to 22 minutes or until top springs back when lightly touched. Cool 1 minute. Carefully remove from pan; place on cooking parchment paper. Cool 10 minutes. Frost with chocolate frosting. Just before serving, dust with powdered sugar; garnish with strawberry slices. Serve warm.

1 Cupcake: Calories 340 (Calories from Fat 150); Total Fat 17g (Saturated Fat 6g); Cholesterol 45mg; Sodium 320mg; Total Carbohydrate 43g (Dietary Fiber 1g)

These warm, gooey cakes are delicious served with a small scoop of vanilla ice cream.

Midnight Marquee Molten Brownie Cupcakes

Prep Time: 10 min ▮ Start to Finish: 30 min ▮ 12 Cupcakes

$^1/_2$ cup semisweet chocolate chips
$^1/_2$ cup butter or margarine
3 eggs
3 egg yolks
1 box (1 lb 6.5 oz) supreme brownie mix with pouch of chocolate flavor syrup
About $^1/_2$ cup stars, confetti or critters decors

1 Heat oven to 400°F. Grease 12 large muffin cups. In medium microwavable bowl, microwave chocolate chips and butter uncovered on High 45 to 60 seconds or until melted and mixture can be stirred smooth.

2 In large bowl, beat eggs and egg yolks with wire whisk or electric mixer until foamy. Reserve chocolate syrup pouch from brownie mix. Gradually beat dry brownie mix into egg mixture until well blended. Gently stir in melted chocolate mixture. Fill muffin cups half full of brownie mixture; top each with ½ teaspoon decors. Top with remaining brownie mixture.

3 Bake 11 to 14 minutes or until edges are set. DO NOT OVERBAKE. Centers will be soft. Cool 2 minutes.

4 Loosen each cupcake with knife; turn upside down onto heatproof tray or cookie sheet. To serve, place cupcake on plate; drizzle with reserved chocolate syrup and top with additional decors.

1 Cupcake: Calories 350 (Calories from Fat 130); Total Fat 15g (Saturated Fat 7g); Cholesterol 125mg; Sodium 240mg; Total Carbohydrate 50g (Dietary Fiber 2g)

Kids will love seeing the shapes oozing out of the molten centers! Use colorful stars, confetti or critter shapes inside cupcakes and also sprinkled on top.

Spring Polka Dot Cupcakes

Rainy Day PB & J Cupcakes

Ring-Around-the-Rosy Cupcakes

May Day Baskets

Flower Pot Cupcakes

Garden Bug Cupcakes

Strawberry–Cream Cheese Cupcakes

Moon and Star Cupcakes

Key West Cupcakes

Piña Colada Cupcakes

S'mores Cupcakes

Spiced Pumpkin Cupcakes

Pistachio Fudge Cups

Minty Fudge Cups

Black and White Rum Cakes

2

seasonal cupcakes

Spring Polka Dot Cupcakes

Prep Time: 40 min ▪ Start to Finish: 1 hr 45 min ▪ 24 Cupcakes

Cupcakes

1 box (1 lb 2.25 oz) white cake mix
    with pudding in the mix
Water, vegetable oil and egg whites
    called for on cake mix box
1 box (4-serving size) orange-
    flavored gelatin

Bright Buttercream Frosting

3 cups powdered sugar
$^1/_3$ cup butter or margarine, softened
1 teaspoon vanilla
2 to 3 tablespoons milk
Yellow, red and blue food colors
$^1/_3$ cup white vanilla baking chips

1 Heat oven to 375°F. Place paper baking cup in each of 24 regular-size muffin cups. In large bowl, beat cake mix, water, oil, egg whites and gelatin with electric mixer on low speed 30 seconds. Beat on medium speed 2 minutes, scraping bowl occasionally. Divide batter evenly among muffin cups.

2 Bake 15 to 20 minutes or until toothpick inserted in center comes out clean. Cool 10 minutes; remove from pan to cooling rack. Cool completely, about 30 minutes.

3 Meanwhile, in medium bowl, beat powdered sugar and butter with spoon or with electric mixer on low speed until well blended. Beat in vanilla and 2 tablespoons milk. Gradually beat in just enough of the remaining milk to make frosting smooth and spreadable. Divide frosting among 4 small bowls. Stir 6 drops yellow food color into frosting in one bowl. Stir 4 drops red food color into frosting in second bowl. Stir 6 to 8 drops blue food color into frosting in third bowl. Stir 4 drops yellow and 2 drops red food color into frosting in fourth bowl.

4 Frost 6 cupcakes with each color of frosting. Poke 4 or 5 white baking chips, flat side up, into frosting on each cupcake to look like polka dots. Store loosely covered at room temperature.

1 Cupcake: Calories 240 (Calories from Fat 80); Total Fat 9g (Saturated Fat 3g); Cholesterol 5mg; Sodium 190mg; Total Carbohydrate 37g (Dietary Fiber 0g)

Have fun making other colors and flavors of cupcakes by using lemon, lime, strawberry, raspberry or watermelon gelatin.

Rainy Day PB & J Cupcakes

Prep Time: 30 min ▪ Start to Finish: 1 hr 40 min ▪ 24 Cupcakes

1 box (1 lb 2.25 oz) yellow cake mix with pudding in the mix
1¼ cups water
¾ cup creamy peanut butter
¼ cup vegetable oil
3 eggs
1 container (12 oz) vanilla whipped ready-to-spread frosting
½ cup creamy peanut butter
2 to 4 tablespoons grape jelly

1 Heat oven to 375°F. Place paper baking cup in each of 24 regular-size muffin cups.

2 In large bowl, beat cake mix, water, ¾ cup peanut butter, the oil and eggs with electric mixer on low speed 30 seconds. Beat on medium speed 1 minute 30 seconds, scraping bowl occasionally. Divide batter evenly among muffin cups.

3 Bake 15 to 20 minutes or until toothpick inserted in center comes out clean. Cool 10 minutes; remove from pan to cooling rack. Cool completely, about 30 minutes.

4 In medium bowl, mix frosting and peanut butter. Frost cupcakes with frosting. Make a small indentation in center of frosting on each cupcake with back of spoon. Just before serving, spoon ¼ to ½ teaspoon jelly into each indentation.

1 Cupcake: Calories 270 (Calories from Fat 120); Total Fat 13g (Saturated Fat 4.5g); Cholesterol 25mg; Sodium 210mg; Total Carbohydrate 32g (Dietary Fiber 1g)

Ring-Around-the-Rosy Cupcakes

Prep Time: 30 min ▪ Start to Finish: 1 hr 45 min ▪ 30 Cupcakes

    Angel Food Cupcakes (page 140)
    Creamy White Frosting (page 149)
    Mini canapé cutters in circles or other shapes
    Colored sugars in desired colors

1 Make Angel Food Cupcakes.

2 Make Creamy White Frosting. Frost cupcakes.

3 Gently press canapé cutter into frosting on cupcake where you want sugar design. Remove cutter and dip bottom edge into one of the sugars, then gently press cutter back into same stamped image on cupcake; remove. Continue with other cutters and colors of sugars.

1 Cupcake (Cake and Frosting): Calories 170 (Calories from Fat 30): Total Fat 3.5g (Saturated Fat 1g); Cholesterol 0mg; Sodium 40mg; Total Carbohydrate 32g (Dietary Fiber 0g)

To add more color, bake these cute cupcakes in decorative baking cups found at cake decorating stores.

May Day Baskets

Prep Time: 20 min   Start to Finish: 1 hr 30 min   24 Cupcakes

1 box (1 lb 2.25 oz) yellow cake mix with pudding in the mix
Water, vegetable oil and eggs called for on cake mix box
1 container (1 lb) creamy ready-to-spread frosting (any flavor) or
    Vanilla Buttercream Frosting (page 146)
Red and blue berry twist licorice
Assorted small candies or jelly beans
Assorted small candies or jelly beans

1 Heat oven to 350°F. Grease bottoms only of 24 regular-size muffin cups with shortening, or line with paper baking cups. Make cake mix as directed on package, using water, oil and eggs. Divide batter evenly among muffin cups.

2 Bake 18 to 23 minutes or until toothpick inserted in center comes out clean. Cool 10 minutes; remove from pan to cooling rack. Cool completely, about 30 minutes.

3 Spread frosting over tops of cupcakes. Make basket handles with licorice. Decorate with candies. Store loosely covered at room temperature.

1 Cupcake: Calories 240 (Calories from Fat 80); Total Fat 9g (Saturated Fat 4g); Cholesterol 25mg; Sodium 170mg; Total Carbohydrate 38g (Dietary Fiber 0g)

Flower Pot Cupcakes

Prep Time: 30 min ▪ Start to Finish: 1 hr 45 min ▪ 24 Cupcakes

Yellow Cupcakes (page 145)
Creamy Vanilla Frosting (page 148)
Red liquid food color
24 scalloped paper baking cups
24 new (clean) small clay flowerpots
1 bag (10.5 oz) pastel-colored miniature marshmallows

1 Bake Yellow Cupcakes as directed for muffin cups to make 24 cupcakes, using scalloped paper baking cups. Make Creamy Vanilla Frosting; tint with 3 drops food color. Frost cupcakes.

2 Place scalloped paper baking cup in each flowerpot, pulling edge of liner over edge of pot. Place cupcakes in flowerpots. Top with mound of marshmallows to look like a chrysanthemum; add 1 marshmallow of different color in center.

1 Cupcake (Cake and Frosting): Calories 290 (Calories from Fat 120); Total Fat 13g (Saturated Fat 5g); Cholesterol 30mg; Sodium 200mg; Total Carbohydrate 40g (Dietary Fiber 2g)

Add planted "flowers" to your cupcake garden.

Gently push flower-shaped candy lollipop into each cupcake. Place piece of green miniature marshmallow at base of lollipop for leaf.

Flower Pot
Cupcakes

Garden Bug
Cupcakes,
page 48

Garden Bug Cupcakes

Prep Time: 30 min ▪ Start to Finish: 1 hr 45 min ▪ 24 Cupcakes

White Cupcakes (page 144)
Creamy Vanilla Frosting (page 148)
Green, purple, blue or red paste or gel food color
Assorted candies (such as round mints, jelly beans, Jordan almonds,
  wafer candies, pieces from candy necklaces)
Miniature marshmallows
Colored sugar
String licorice
1 tube (4.25 oz) white decorating icing

1 Bake White Cupcakes as directed for muffin cups to make 24 cupcakes. Make Creamy Vanilla Frosting. Tint frosting with desired food color; frost cupcakes.

2 Arrange candies on cupcakes to make bug heads, bodies and wings. In addition to candies, use whole marshmallows or sliced marshmallows sprinkled with colored sugar. Use pieces of licorice for antennae. For eyes, add dots of decorating icing.

1 Cupcake (Cake and Frosting): Calories 320 (Calories from Fat 100); Total Fat 11g (Saturated Fat 4g); Cholesterol 15mg; Sodium 220mg; Total Carbohydrate 51g (Dietary Fiber 0g)

As a special touch for a kids' party, have the cupcakes baked and frosted. Set out dishes of decorating candies and tubes of decorating gel, and let the kids create their own bugs.

Photo, page 47.

Strawberry–Cream Cheese Cupcakes

Prep Time: 20 min ▪ Start to Finish: 1 hr 25 min ▪ 24 Cupcakes

1 box (1 lb 2.25 oz) yellow cake mix with pudding in the mix
1 container (8 oz) sour cream
1/2 cup vegetable oil
1/2 cup water
2 eggs
3 tablespoons strawberry preserves
1 package (3 oz) cream cheese, cut into 24 pieces
1 container (1 lb) cream cheese creamy ready-to-spread frosting
Sliced fresh small strawberries, if desired

1 Heat oven to 350°F. Place paper baking cup in each of 24 regular-size muffin cups. In large bowl, mix cake mix, sour cream, oil, water and eggs with spoon until well blended (batter will be thick). Divide batter evenly among muffin cups.

2 In small bowl, place strawberry preserves; stir until smooth. Place 1 piece of cream cheese on top of batter in each cupcake; press in slightly. Place 1/4 measuring teaspoon of preserves over cream cheese.

3 Bake 18 to 23 minutes or until tops are golden brown and spring back when touched lightly in center (some preserves may show in tops of cupcakes). Cool 10 minutes; remove from pan to cooling rack. Cool completely, about 30 minutes.

4 Frost with frosting. Just before serving, garnish with strawberry slices. Store covered in refrigerator.

1 Cupcake: Calories 265 (Calories from Fat 135); Total Fat 15g (Saturated Fat 5g); Cholesterol 30mg; Sodium 200mg; Total Carbohydrate 31g (Dietary Fiber 0g)

Moon and Star Cupcakes

Prep Time: 35 min ■ Start to Finish: 1 hr 50 min ■ 24 Cupcakes

Yellow Cupcakes (page 145)
Creamy White Frosting (page 149)
Blue paste or gel food color
White edible glitter, decorator sugar crystals or candy sprinkles
Large yellow gumdrops
Large white gumdrops

1 Bake Yellow Cupcakes as directed for muffin cups to make 24 cupcakes. Make Creamy White Frosting; tint with food color to make blue. Frost cupcakes. Sprinkle with edible glitter.

2 To make moons and stars, on piece of waxed paper, flatten gumdrops with rolling pin until 1⅞ inches in diameter (sprinkle with sugar to keep from sticking). From yellow gumdrops, cut out crescent shapes with small sharp knife or small cookie cutter. From white gumdrops, cut out star shapes. Place on cupcake, inserting toothpick if needed to prop up.

1 Cupcake (Cake and Frosting): Calories 260 (Calories from Fat 100); Total Fat 11g (Saturated Fat 5g); Cholesterol 50mg; Sodium 240mg; Total Carbohydrate 38g (Dietary Fiber 0g)

Let the sun come out! Tint 2 containers (1 pound each) creamy white frosting with yellow food color; frost cupcakes. Decorate with candy corn to make outline of sun, and create a face with colorful candies.

Key West Cupcakes

Prep Time: 25 min ▪ Start to Finish: 1 hr 30 min ▪ 24 Cupcakes

Key Lime Filling

1 box (4-serving size) vanilla instant pudding and pie filling mix

1^1/$_2$ cups whipping cream

^{1}/$_4$ cup fresh Key lime or regular lime juice

4 drops green food color

1^1/$_2$ cups powdered sugar

Cupcakes

1 box (1 lb 2.25 oz) yellow cake mix with pudding in the mix

Water, vegetable oil and eggs called for on cake mix box

Key Lime Frosting

1 container (12 oz) fluffy white whipped ready-to-spread frosting

1 tablespoon fresh Key lime or regular lime juice

^{1}/$_2$ teaspoon grated Key lime or regular lime peel

1 In large bowl, beat pudding mix and whipping cream with wire whisk 2 minutes. Let stand 3 minutes. Beat in ¼ cup lime juice and the food color; stir in powdered sugar until smooth. Cover; refrigerate.

2 Heat oven to 350°F. Place paper baking cup in each of 24 regular-size muffin cups. Make and bake cake mix as directed on box for 24 cupcakes, using water, oil and eggs. Cool 10 minutes; remove from pan to cooling rack. Cool completely, about 30 minutes.

3 Spread 1 rounded tablespoonful filling on top of each cupcake. Stir frosting in container 20 times. Gently stir in 1 tablespoon lime juice and the lime peel. Spoon frosting into 1-quart resealable food-storage plastic bag. Cut ½-inch tip from 1 bottom corner of bag. Squeeze 1 tablespoon frosting from bag onto filling on each cupcake. Store covered in refrigerator.

1 Cupcake: Calories 280 (Calories from Fat 120); Total Fat 13g (Saturated Fat 5g); Cholesterol 45mg; Sodium 230mg; Total Carbohydrate 38g (Dietary Fiber 0g)

Love lemon? Use fresh lemon juice for the lime juice, lemon peel for the lime peel and yellow food color for the green.

Piña Colada Cupcakes

Prep Time: 20 min ▪ Start to Finish: 1 hr 40 min ▪ 24 Cupcakes

1 box (1 lb 2.25 oz) yellow cake mix with pudding in the mix
$^1/_3$ cup vegetable oil
$^1/_4$ cup water
1 teaspoon rum extract
1 can (8 oz) crushed pineapple in juice, undrained
3 eggs
1 teaspoon coconut extract
1 teaspoon rum extract
1 container (12 oz) whipped vanilla ready-to-spread frosting
$^3/_4$ cup shredded coconut

1 Heat oven to 375°F. Place paper baking cup in each of 24 regular-size muffin cups. In large bowl, beat cake mix, oil, water, 1 teaspoon rum extract, pineapple and eggs with electric mixer on low speed 30 seconds. Beat on medium speed 2 minutes, scraping bowl occasionally. Divide batter evenly among muffin cups.

2 Bake 14 to 19 minutes or until toothpick inserted in center comes out clean. Cool 10 minutes; remove from pan to cooling rack. Cool completely, about 30 minutes.

3 Stir coconut extract and 1 teaspoon rum extract into frosting. Spread frosting on cupcakes. Dip tops of frosted cupcakes in coconut. Store loosely covered at room temperature.

1 Cupcake: Calories 210 (Calories from Fat 80); Total Fat 9g (Saturated Fat 3g); Cholesterol 25mg; Sodium 170mg; Total Carbohydrate 29g (Dietary Fiber 0g)

S'mores Cupcakes

Prep Time: 45 min ▪ Start to Finish: 2 hr ▪ 24 Cupcakes

Cupcakes

1 box (1 lb 2.25 oz) yellow cake mix with pudding in the mix

Water, vegetable oil and eggs called for on cake mix box

1 cup graham cracker crumbs

4 bars (1.55 oz each) milk chocolate candy, finely chopped

Frosting

1 jar (7 oz) marshmallow creme

½ cup butter or margarine, softened

2 cups powdered sugar

1 to 2 teaspoons milk

1 bar (1.55 oz) milk chocolate candy, if desired

24 teddy bear–shaped graham snacks, if desired

1 Heat oven to 375°F. Place paper baking cup in each of 24 regular-size muffin cups. In large bowl, beat cake mix, water, oil and eggs with electric mixer on low speed 30 seconds. Beat on medium speed 2 minutes, scraping bowl occasionally. Fold in graham cracker crumbs and chopped chocolate bars. Divide batter evenly among muffin cups.

2 Bake 20 to 24 minutes or until toothpick inserted in center comes out clean. Cool 10 minutes; remove from pan to cooling rack. Cool completely, about 30 minutes.

3 Remove lid and foil seal from jar of marshmallow creme. Microwave on High 15 to 20 seconds. In large bowl, beat marshmallow creme, butter and powdered sugar on low speed until blended. Beat in enough milk, ½ teaspoon at a time, to make frosting spreadable. Spread over tops of cupcakes.

4 Divide chocolate bar into rectangles. Cut each rectangle diagonally in half and place on top of each cupcake. Top each cupcake with teddy bear–shaped snack. After frosting has set, store loosely covered at room temperature.

1 Cupcake: Calories 280 (Calories from Fat 110); Total Fat 12g (Saturated Fat 5g); Cholesterol 40mg; Sodium 210mg; Total Carbohydrate 41g (Dietary Fiber 0g)

To keep the chocolate from sinking into the cake batter, chop it finely.

Spiced Pumpkin Cupcakes

Prep Time: 40 min ▪ Start to Finish: 1 hr 40 min ▪ 24 Cupcakes

1/2 cup finely chopped pecans
3 tablespoons sugar
1 box (1 lb 2.25 oz) yellow cake mix with pudding in the mix
1 cup pumpkin from 15-oz can (not pumpkin pie mix)
1/2 cup water
1/3 cup vegetable oil
4 eggs
1 1/2 teaspoons pumpkin pie spice
1 container (1 lb) cream cheese creamy ready-to-spread frosting

1 Heat oven to 350°F. Place paper baking cup in each of 24 regular-size muffin cups.

2 In heavy 8-inch nonstick skillet, cook pecans and 2 tablespoons of the sugar over low heat about 8 minutes, stirring constantly, until sugar is melted. Spoon and spread pecans onto sheet of waxed paper. Sprinkle with remaining 1 tablespoon sugar; toss.

3 In large bowl, beat cake mix, pumpkin, water, oil, eggs and pumpkin pie spice with electric mixer on low speed 30 seconds. Beat on medium speed 2 minutes, scraping bowl occasionally. Divide batter evenly among muffin cups.

4 Bake 20 to 25 minutes or until toothpick inserted in center comes out clean. Cool 10 minutes; remove from pan to cooling rack. Cool completely, about 30 minutes.

5 Frost cupcakes with frosting. Sprinkle edge of frosted cupcakes with pecans; press lightly into frosting.

1 Cupcake: Calories 230 (Calories from Fat 90); Total Fat 10g (Saturated Fat 2g); Cholesterol 35mg; Sodium 210mg; Total Carbohydrate 34g (Dietary Fiber 0g)

Use a heavy skillet, low heat and a constant eye to cook the sugar and nuts to ensure no burning.

Pistachio Fudge Cups

Prep Time: 25 min ▪ Start to Finish: 45 min ▪ 24 Cups

Crust
1/4 cup butter or margarine,
   softened
1 package (3 oz) cream cheese,
   softened
3/4 cup all-purpose flour
1/4 cup powdered sugar
2 tablespoons unsweetened
   baking cocoa

1/2 teaspoon vanilla
Pistachio Fudge Filling
2/3 cup granulated sugar
2/3 cup chopped pistachio nuts
1/3 cup unsweetened baking cocoa
2 tablespoons butter or margarine,
   softened
1 egg

1 Heat oven to 350°F. In large bowl, beat butter and cream cheese with electric mixer on medium speed, or mix with spoon. Stir in remaining crust ingredients until well blended.

2 Divide dough into 24 equal pieces. Press each piece in bottom and up side of ungreased mini muffin cup.

3 In medium bowl, mix all filling ingredients until well blended. Spoon about 2 teaspoons filling into each cup.

4 Bake 18 to 20 minutes or until almost no indentation remains when filling is touched lightly. Cool slightly; loosen from muffin cups with tip of knife. Remove from pan to cooling rack.

1 Cup: Calories 115 (Calories from Fat 65); Total Fat 7g (Saturated Fat 3g); Cholesterol 20mg; Sodium 60mg; Total Carbohydrate 12g (Dietary Fiber 1g)

Bake these gems in sparkling gold or silver baking cups, and swirl on your favorite frosting.

Minty Fudge Cups

Prep Time: 30 min ▪ Start to Finish: 1 hr 20 min ▪ 24 Fudge cups

Topping
1 package (4.67 oz) rectangular
  chocolate mints, unwrapped

Minty Fudge Filling
²/₃ cup granulated sugar
¹/₃ cup unsweetened baking cocoa
2 tablespoons butter or margarine,
  softened
1 egg
Reserved ¹/₂ cup coarsely chopped
  mints

Fudge Cups
¹/₄ cup butter or margarine,
  softened
1 package (3 oz) cream cheese,
  softened
³/₄ cup all-purpose flour
¹/₄ cup powdered sugar
2 tablespoons unsweetened baking cocoa
¹/₂ teaspoon vanilla
1 container (1 lb) chocolate creamy
  ready-to-spread frosting

1 Heat oven to 350°F. Place paper baking cup in each of 24 mini muffin cups. Coarsely chop enough mints (about 15) to measure ½ cup; reserve for filling. Coarsely chop remaining mints for topping; set aside.

2 In small bowl, beat all filling ingredients except chopped mints with spoon until well mixed; stir in mints.

3 In large bowl, beat ¼ cup butter and the cream cheese with electric mixer on medium speed, or mix with spoon. Stir in flour, powdered sugar, 2 tablespoons cocoa and the vanilla.

4 Shape dough into 1-inch balls. Press each ball in bottom and up side of each muffin cup. Spoon about 2 teaspoons filling into each cup.

5 Bake 18 to 20 minutes or until almost no indentation remains when filling is touched lightly. Cool slightly; carefully remove from muffin cups to cooling rack. Cool completely, about 30 minutes. Frost with frosting. Sprinkle with remaining chopped mints.

1 Fudge Cup: Calories 205 (Calories from Fat 100); Total Fat 11g (Saturated Fat 7g); Cholesterol 20mg; Sodium 40mg; Total Carbohydrate 25g (Dietary Fiber 1g)

Black and White Rum Cakes

Prep Time: 55 min ▪ Start to Finish: 2 hr ▪ 24 Cupcakes

Cupcakes

1 box (1 lb 2.25 oz) white cake mix
with pudding in the mix

1¼ cups water

⅓ cup vegetable oil

3 eggs

3 oz unsweetened baking
chocolate, melted, cooled

2 teaspoons rum extract

Rum Frosting and Garnish

2 egg whites

½ cup sugar

¼ cup light corn syrup

2 tablespoons water

2 teaspoons rum extract

Chocolate candy sprinkles

1 Heat oven to 375°F. Place paper baking cup in each of 24 regular-size muffin cups. In large bowl, beat cake mix, water, oil and eggs with electric mixer on low speed 30 seconds. Beat on medium speed 2 minutes, scraping bowl occasionally.

2 In small bowl, place 2 cups of the batter; stir in chocolate. Into remaining batter, stir 2 teaspoons rum extract. Into bottom of each muffin cup, spoon about 1½ tablespoons chocolate batter. Top each with about 1½ tablespoons rum batter.

3 Bake 15 to 20 minutes or until toothpick inserted in center comes out clean. Cool 10 minutes; remove from pan to cooling rack. Cool completely, about 30 minutes.

4 In medium bowl, beat 2 egg whites with electric mixer on high speed just until stiff peaks form; set aside.

5 In 1-quart saucepan, stir sugar, corn syrup and 2 tablespoons water until well mixed. Cover and heat to rolling boil over medium heat. Uncover and boil 4 to 8 minutes, without stirring, to 242°F on candy thermometer or until small amount of mixture dropped into cup of very cold water forms a firm ball that holds its shape until pressed. For an accurate temperature reading, tilt the saucepan slightly so mixture is deep enough for thermometer.

6 Pour hot syrup very slowly in thin stream into egg whites, beating constantly on medium speed. Add 2 teaspoons rum extract. Beat on high speed about 10 minutes or until stiff peaks form. Immediately frost cupcakes. Sprinkle half of cupcake with chocolate sprinkles. Store in refrigerator.

1 Cupcake: Calories 180 (Calories from Fat 70); Total Fat 8g (Saturated Fat 2.5g); Cholesterol 25mg; Sodium 160mg; Total Carbohydrate 25g (Dietary Fiber 0g)

Punch up these rum-flavored treats with a scoop of rum-raisin ice cream.

All-Star Cupcakes

Confetti Party Cupcakes

Happy Birthday Marshmallow Cupcakes

Easy Birthday Cupcakes

Mini Cupcake Mortarboards

Graduation Cupcakes

Wedding Cupcakes

Almond Baby Cakes

Baby Bootie Shower Cakes

Cherry Mini Cakes

"Just Because" Cream-Filled Cupcakes

Anniversary White Truffle Cupcakes

Truffle Lover's Cupcakes

3

celebration cupcakes

All-Star Cupcakes

Prep Time: 40 min ▪ Start to Finish: 1 hr 40 min ▪ 24 Cupcakes

1 box (1 lb 2.25 oz) white cake mix
 with pudding in the mix
1¼ cups water
⅓ cup vegetable oil
½ teaspoon almond extract
3 egg whites

1 container (1 lb) vanilla creamy
 ready-to-spread frosting
Blue paste food color
¼ cup blue candy sprinkles or
 colored sugar
2 oz vanilla-flavored candy coating
 (almond bark)

1 Heat oven to 375°F. Place paper baking cup in each of 24 regular-size muffin cups. In large bowl, beat cake mix, water, oil, almond extract and egg whites with electric mixer on low speed 30 seconds. Beat on medium speed 2 minutes, scraping bowl occasionally. Divide batter evenly among muffin cups.

2 Bake 15 to 20 minutes or until toothpick inserted in center comes out clean. Cool in pan 10 minutes; remove from pan to cooling rack. Cool completely, about 30 minutes.

3 In small bowl, place half of frosting. Dip toothpick into paste food color; stir into frosting to reach desired shade. Frost 12 cupcakes with blue frosting. Frost remaining 12 cupcakes with white frosting; sprinkle blue candy sprinkles over white cupcakes.

4 Chop candy coating; place in small microwaveable bowl. Microwave uncovered on High 30 seconds; stir until melted and smooth. If necessary, microwave an additional 10 seconds. Place in heavy-duty food storage plastic bag; cut tiny tip off 1 bottom corner of bag.

5 On piece of paper, draw free-form 5-pointed star, about 2 inches wide, to use as pattern. Place pattern under large sheet of waxed paper. Squeezing bag of candy coating, trace the star on waxed paper; move pattern under waxed paper to make 12 stars. Let stand about 5 minutes or until candy coating is set. Remove stars from waxed paper; gently insert in each of 12 cupcakes.

1 Cupcake: Calories 220 (Calories from Fat 90g); Total Fat 10g (Saturated Fat 3g); Cholesterol 0mg; Sodium 200mg; Total Carbohydrate 32g (Dietary Fiber 0g)

Confetti Party Cupcakes

Prep Time: 30 min ▪ Start to Finish: 1 hr 45 min ▪ 12 Servings

1 box (1 lb 2.25 oz) cake mix with pudding in the mix (any flavor)
Water, vegetable oil and eggs called for on cake mix box
1 container (12 oz) fluffy white whipped ready-to-spread frosting or 1 container
   (1 lb) vanilla creamy ready-to-spread frosting
Yellow, red and blue gel food colors
Candy sprinkles or decors, as desired

1 Heat oven to 350°F. Spray bottom and side of 1 (9-inch) round cake pan with baking spray with flour. Place paper baking cups in each of 12 regular-size muffin cups.

2 Make cake as directed on box, using water, oil and eggs. Spread half the batter in round pan; divide remaining batter evenly among muffin cups. Bake as directed on box for 9-inch round pan and cupcakes. Cool 10 minutes; remove from pans to cooling racks. Cool completely, about 1 hour.

3 In small bowl, place 1 tablespoon frosting; stir in 1 drop yellow food color. In another small bowl, place ¼ cup frosting; stir in 2 drops red food color. In third small bowl, place ½ cup frosting; stir in 4 drops blue food color.

4 On serving plate, place cake layer with rounded side down. Frost top and side with white frosting. Frost 7 cupcakes with blue frosting, 4 cupcakes with pink frosting and 1 cupcake with yellow frosting. Place 1 blue cupcake on center of white frosted cake. Place remaining blue cupcakes, sides touching, in circle around center cupcake. Place 2 rows of 2 pink cupcakes on top center of blue cupcakes. Place yellow cupcake on top center. Sprinkle with candy sprinkles. Store loosely covered at room temperature.

1 Serving: Calories 370 (Calories from Fat 150); Total Fat 17g (Saturated Fat 4.5g); Cholesterol 55mg; Sodium 330mg; Total Carbohydrate 53g (Dietary Fiber 0g)

Happy Birthday Marshmallow Cupcakes

Prep Time: 30 min ▪ Start to Finish: 1 hr 45 min ▪ 24 Cupcakes

White Cupcakes (page 144)
Creamy Vanilla Frosting (page 148)
24 to 30 large marshmallows
Colored sugar or candy sprinkles
White or colored birthday candles

1 Bake White Cupcakes as directed for muffin cups to make 24 cupcakes. Make Creamy Vanilla Frosting; frost cupcakes.

2 Cut marshmallows with dampened kitchen scissors into slices; sprinkle with colored sugar. Arrange on cupcakes in flower shape. Place candle in middle of each flower.

1 Cupcake (Cake and Frosting): Calories 360 (Calories from Fat 110); Total Fat 12g (Saturated Fat 4.5g); Cholesterol 15mg; Sodium 240mg; Total Carbohydrates 61g (Dietary Fiber 0g)

Easy Birthday Cupcakes

Prep Time: 10 min ▪ Start to Finish: 1 hr 20 min ▪ 24 Cupcakes

1 box (1 lb 2.25 oz) yellow cake mix with pudding in the mix
Water, vegetable oil and eggs called for on cake mix box
1 container (1 lb) creamy white ready-to-spread frosting
24 ring-shaped hard candies or jelly beans, if desired
Assorted small colorful candies and sugars, if desired

1 Heat oven to 350°F. Place paper baking cup in each of 24 regular-size muffin cups. Make cake mix as directed on box, using water, oil and eggs. Divide batter evenly among muffin cups.

2 Bake 21 to 26 minutes or until toothpick inserted in center comes out clean. Cool 10 minutes; remove from pan to cooling rack. Cool completely, about 30 minutes.

3 Frost cupcakes with frosting. Use ring candies as candleholders. Decorate with assorted candies. Store loosely covered at room temperature.

1 Cupcake: Calories 220 (Calories from Fat 90); Total Fat 10g (Saturated Fat 3g); Cholesterol 25mg; Sodium 200mg; Total Carbohydrate 31g (Dietary Fiber 0g)

Mini Cupcake Mortarboards

Prep Time: 30 min ▪ Start to Finish: 1 hr 45 min ▪ 60 Mortarboards

1 box (1 lb 2.25 oz) cake mix with pudding in the mix (any flavor)
Water, vegetable oil and eggs called for on cake mix box
1 package (4.5 oz) chewy fruit snack in 3-foot rolls (any flavor)
1 container (1 lb) vanilla creamy ready-to-spread frosting
60 square shortbread cookies (from two 10-oz packages)
60 candy-coated chocolate or fruit-flavored candies

1 Heat oven to 350°F. Line 24 mini muffin cups with mini paper baking cups. Make cake mix as directed on package, using water, oil and eggs. Fill cups ⅔ full (about 1 rounded tablespoon each). Refrigerate remaining batter.

2 Bake 15 to 20 minutes or until toothpick inserted in center comes out clean. Remove from pan to cooling rack. Cool completely. Meanwhile, repeat with remaining batter to make a total of 60 mini cupcakes.

3 To make tassels, cut sixty 2½-inch lengths from fruit snack rolls. Cut each length into several strips up to ½ inch from one end. Roll uncut end between fingertips to make fringes on ends of tassels.

4 Frost bottoms of cookies. Turn cupcakes in paper baking cups upside down. For each mortarboard, place small dollop of frosting on bottom of cupcake; top with cookie. Press uncut end of fruit snack into frosted cookie. Place 1 candy on frosted cookie next to tassel. Store loosely covered at room temperature.

1 Mortarboard: Calories 140 (Calories from Fat 55); Total Fat 6g (Saturated Fat 2g); Cholesterol 15mg; Sodium 110mg; Total Carbohydrate 20g (Dietary Fiber 0g)

Graduation Cupcakes

Prep Time: 35 min ▮ Start to Finish: 1 hr 50 min ▮ 24 Cupcakes

2 rolls chewy fruit snack in 3-foot rolls, any flavor (from 4.5-oz box)
1 box (1 lb 2.25 oz) cake mix with pudding in the mix (any flavor)
Water, vegetable oil and eggs called for on cake mix box
2 containers (12 oz each) fluffy white whipped ready-to-spread frosting
Food color, if desired
Decorating gel (from 0.68-oz tube) in any color
Candy sprinkles, if desired
Colored sugar, if desired
Additional rolls of chewy fruit snack in 3-foot rolls, if desired
Miniature chocolate-covered peanut butter cup candies, if desired
Fudge-covered graham crackers, if desired

1 Cut fruit snack rolls into 12-inch pieces. Cut each piece lengthwise into 4 strips, using knife and straightedge. Roll each strip in a spiral around handle of wooden spoon. Store at room temperature at least 8 hours to set curl.

2 Make and bake cake as directed on box for 24 cupcakes, using water, oil and eggs. Cool 10 minutes; remove from pan to cooling rack. Cool completely, about 30 minutes.

3 Tint half of frosting with food color. Frost cupcakes with frosting. Write "Congratulations" or "Congrats" and the graduate's name on cupcakes (one letter per cupcake) with decorating gel. Decorate other cupcakes with candy sprinkles and colored sugar. Unwrap fruit snack streamers from spoon handles. Reshape into desired curl; place on cupcakes. Cut additional fruit snack into small pieces and flower petal shapes; arrange on some of the cupcakes.

4 Top some of the cupcakes with candy graduation caps. To make, place small amount of frosting on bottom of peanut butter cup. Press graham cracker onto peanut butter cup. To make tassel, tightly roll up small square of chewy fruit snack; cut fringe in one end and press other end to center of graham cracker.

1 Cupcake (Cake and Frosting): Calories 250 (Calories from Fat 110); Total Fat 12g (Saturated Fat 3g); Cholesterol 25mg; Sodium 180mg; Total Carbohydrate 35g (Dietary Fiber 0g)

Change it up! To celebrate a special anniversary, write "Happy Anniversary" on the cupcakes.

Wedding Cupcakes

Prep Time: 45 min ▪ Start to Finish: 2 hrs ▪ 24 Cupcakes

White Cupcakes (page 144)
White paper baking cups
Creamy Vanilla Frosting (page 148)

Decorating Options
White Chocolate Curls (below)

Pink rose petals
Handmade paper, cut into 8 x
1¼-inch strips
Decorator sugar crystals or edible
glitter
Ribbon

1 Bake White Cupcakes as directed for muffin cups to make 24 cupcakes, using white paper baking cups. Make Creamy Vanilla Frosting; frost cupcakes.

2 Choose from these decorating options:

▪ Top cupcakes with White Chocolate Curls (below) or rose petals.

▪ Wrap handmade paper around each cupcake; attach with permanent double-stick tape.

▪ Sprinkle decorator sugar crystals or edible glitter over frosting.

▪ Wrap ribbon around each cupcake and tie in a bow.

1 Cupcake (Cake and Frosting): Calories 320 (Calories from Fat 100); Total Fat 11g (Saturated Fat 4g); Cholesterol 15mg; Sodium 220mg; Total Carbohydrate 51g (Dietary Fiber 0g)

White Chocolate Curls: Place bar of room-temperature white chocolate on waxed paper. Make curls by pulling a vegetable peeler toward you in long, thin strokes while pressing firmly against the chocolate. (If curls crumble or stay too straight, chocolate may be too cold; placing the heel of your hand on the chocolate will warm it enough to get good curls.) Transfer each curl carefully with a toothpick to a waxed paper–lined cookie sheet or directly onto frosted cupcake.

Almond Baby Cakes

Prep Time: 1 hr 50 min ▮ Start to Finish: 1 hr 50 min ▮ 60 Baby cakes

1 box (1 lb 2.25 oz) white cake mix with pudding in the mix
1¼ cups water
⅓ cup vegetable oil
1 teaspoon almond extract
3 egg whites
Petits Fours Glaze (page 153)
Assorted colors decorating icing (in 4.25-oz tubes)

1 Heat oven to 375°F. Grease bottoms only of about 60 mini muffin cups with shortening or baking spray. In large bowl, beat cake mix, water, oil, almond extract and egg whites with electric mixer on low speed 30 seconds. Beat on medium speed 2 minutes, scraping bowl occasionally. Divide batter evenly among muffin cups (about ½ full). (If using one pan, refrigerate batter while baking other cakes; wash pan before filling with additional batter.)

2 Bake 10 to 15 minutes or until toothpick inserted in center comes out clean. Cool 5 minutes; remove from pan to cooling rack. Cool completely, about 30 minutes.

3 Make Petits Fours Glaze. Place cooling rack on cookie sheet or waxed paper to catch glaze drips. Turn each baby cake on cooling rack so top side is down. Pour about 1 tablespoon glaze over each cake, letting glaze coat the sides. Let stand 15 minutes.

4 With decorating icing, pipe designs on cakes in shapes of letters, animals, safety pins, booties, rattles or bottles. Store loosely covered at room temperature.

1 Baby Cake (Cake and Frosting): Calories 120 (Calories from Fat 20): Total Fat 2g (Saturated Fat 0g); Cholesterol 0mg; Sodium 65mg; Total Carbohydrate 24g (Dietary Fiber 0g)

Bake the baby cakes up to 2 weeks ahead of time. Freeze, then add the glaze and decorate right before the party.

Baby Bootie Shower Cakes

Prep Time: 40 min ▮ Start to Finish: 1 hr 55 min ▮ 16 Booties

White Cupcakes (page 144)   Decorating bag with tips
White Mountain Frosting (page 150)   Striped fruit-flavored gum
Food colors, if desired

1 Bake White Cupcakes as directed for 24 regular-size muffin cups to make cupcakes. Remove paper baking cups if used. Place 2 cupcakes upside down on separate plates. Cut small piece off side of a third cupcake to form flat surface. Cut third cupcake horizontally in half. Place one half with cut side against cupcake on plate to form bootie as shown in diagram. Place remaining half against second cupcake. Repeat with remaining cupcakes.

2 Make White Mountain Frosting; reserve ⅔ cup. Tint remaining frosting with food color if desired. Frost booties, attaching pieces with small amount of frosting. Place reserved frosting in decorating bag with writing tip #4. Outline top and tongue of booties with frosting. Cut gum into strips for accents and lace; place on booties.

1 Bootie (Cake and Frosting): Calories 280 (Calories from Fat 80); Total Fat 9g (Saturated Fat 2.5g); Cholesterol 0mg; Sodium 290mg; Total Carbohydrate 46g (Dietary Fiber 0g)

For a traditional look, tint the booties pastel yellow, blue or pink. For a fun, contemporary look, use bright primary colors.

Cutting and Assembling Bootie Shower Cakes: (1) Cut piece off side of one cupcake. (2) Cut cupcake horizontally in half. (3) Place halves with cut sides against two other cupcakes.

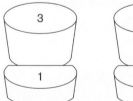

Cherry Mini Cakes

Prep Time: 1 hr 50 min ▪ Start to Finish: 1 hr 50 min ▪ 60 Mini cakes

Mini Cakes	**Glaze and Decoration**
1 box (1 lb 2.25 oz) white cake mix with pudding in the mix	1 bag (2 lb) powdered sugar (8 cups)
1 package (0.14 oz) cherry-flavored unsweetened soft drink mix	$1/2$ cup water
$1^1/_4$ cups water	$1/2$ cup corn syrup
$1/_3$ cup vegetable oil	2 teaspoons almond extract
1 teaspoon almond extract	2 to 3 teaspoons hot water
3 egg whites	Miniature red candy hearts

1 Heat oven to 375°F. Grease bottoms only of about 60 mini muffin cups with shortening or cooking spray. In large bowl, beat all mini cakes ingredients with electric mixer on low speed 30 seconds. Beat on medium speed 2 minutes, scraping bowl occasionally.

2 Divide batter evenly among muffin cups. (If using one pan, refrigerate batter while baking other cakes; wash pan before filling with additional batter.)

3 Bake 10 to 13 minutes or until toothpick inserted in center comes out clean. Cool 5 minutes; remove from pan to cooling rack. Cool completely, about 30 minutes.

4 Place cooling rack on cookie sheet or waxed paper to catch glaze drips. In 3-quart saucepan, mix all glaze ingredients except hot water and candy hearts. Heat over low heat, stirring frequently, until sugar is dissolved. Remove from heat. Stir in 2 teaspoons hot water. If necessary, stir in up to 1 teaspoon more water so glaze will just coat cakes.

5 Turn each cake so top side is down on cooling rack. Pour about 1 tablespoon glaze over each cake, letting glaze coat sides. Let stand until glaze is set, about 15 minutes.

6 Top each cake with hearts. Store loosely covered.

1 Mini Cake: Calories 120 (Calories from Fat 20); Total Fat 2g (Saturated Fat 0g); Cholesterol 0mg; Sodium 65mg; Total Carbohydrate 25g (Dietary Fiber 0g)

"Just Because" Cream-Filled Cupcakes

Prep Time: 30 min ▪ Start to Finish: 1 hr 15 min ▪ 24 Cupcakes

> 1 box (1 lb 2.25 oz) devil's food cake mix with pudding in the mix
> Water, vegetable oil and eggs called for on cake mix box
> 1½ containers (12 oz each) fluffy white whipped ready-to-spread frosting
> ½ cup miniature semisweet chocolate chips

1 Heat oven to 350°F. Make and bake cake mix as directed on box for 24 cupcakes, using water, oil and eggs. Cool 10 minutes; remove from pan to cooling racks. Cool completely, about 30 minutes.

2 Spoon frosting into corner of resealable heavy-duty food-storage plastic bag. Cut about ¼ inch tip off 1 bottom corner of bag. Gently push cut corner of bag into center of cupcake. Squeeze about 2 teaspoons frosting into center of each cupcake for filling, being careful not to split cupcake. Frost tops of cupcakes with remaining frosting.

3 Sprinkle chocolate chips on top of each cupcake. Store loosely covered.

1 Cupcake: Calories 250 (Calories from Fat 110); Total Fat 12g (Saturated Fat 3.5g); Cholesterol 25mg; Sodium 200mg; Total Carbohydrate 33g (Dietary Fiber 0g)

Anniversary White Truffle Cupcakes

Prep Time: 35 min ▮ Start to Finish: 1 hr 10 min ▮ 24 Cupcakes

> 1 box (1 lb 2.25 oz) devil's food cake mix with pudding in the mix
> Water, vegetable oil and eggs called for on cake mix box
> 1 cup white vanilla baking chips (6 oz)
> 1 container (1 lb) vanilla or chocolate creamy ready-to-spread frosting
> Ribbon, if desired

1 Heat oven to 350°F. Place paper baking cup in each of 24 regular-size muffin cups. Make and bake cake as directed on box for 24 cupcakes, using water, oil and eggs. Cool 10 minutes; remove from pan to cooling rack. Cool completely, about 30 minutes.

2 In medium microwavable bowl, microwave vanilla chips uncovered on Medium 4 to 5 minutes, stirring after 2 minutes. Stir until smooth; cool 5 minutes. Stir in frosting until well blended. Immediately frost cupcakes or pipe frosting on cupcakes.

3 Tie ribbons around cupcakes for decoration (see cover photo). Store loosely covered.

1 Cupcake: Calories 270 (Calories from Fat 120); Total Fat 13g (Saturated Fat 5g); Cholesterol 25mg; Sodium 240mg; Total Carbohydrate 36g (Dietary Fiber 0g)

For a touch that's "from the heart," place melted and cooled dark or white chocolate in a plastic food storage bag. Cut the tip off one corner and pipe heart shapes onto wax paper. Refrigerate to harden, then carefully place on cupcakes.

Truffle Lover's Cupcakes

Prep Time: 35 min ▪ Start to Finish: 2 hr 10 min ▪ 24 Cupcakes

Cupcakes
1 box (1 lb 2.25 oz) chocolate fudge
    cake mix with pudding in the mix
Water, vegetable oil and eggs called
    for on cake mix box
1/4 cup mini semisweet chocolate
    chips
1/3 cup hazelnuts, toasted and ground*

1 teaspoon grated orange peel
4 teaspoons hazelnut liqueur
4 teaspoons orange-flavored liqueur
Ganache
1/3 cup whipping cream
1/2 cup semisweet chocolate chips
Mini semisweet chocolate chips
Additional grated orange peel

1 Heat oven to 375°F. Place paper baking cup in each of 24 regular-size muffin cups (use 8 each of 3 different colors).

2 In large bowl, beat cake mix, water, oil and eggs with electric mixer on low speed 1 minute, scraping bowl constantly. Divide batter among three bowls. Stir 1/4 cup mini chocolate chips into one bowl; spoon into 8 muffin cups of same color.

3 Reserve 2 tablespoons ground hazelnuts. Stir remaining hazelnuts into second bowl; spoon into 8 muffin cups of second color. Stir 1 teaspoon grated orange peel into remaining batter; spoon into remaining muffin cups.

4 Bake 21 to 26 minutes or until toothpick inserted in center comes out clean. Cool 10 minutes; remove from pan to cooling rack. Prick holes in tops of hazelnut and orange cupcakes with toothpick. Brush 1/2 teaspoon hazelnut liqueur over each hazelnut cupcake; brush 1/2 teaspoon orange liqueur over each orange cupcake. Cool completely, about 30 minutes.

5 In heavy 1-quart saucepan, heat whipping cream over medium-high heat until hot but not boiling; remove from heat. Stir in 1/2 cup chocolate chips until melted. Let stand 5 minutes. Dip tops of cupcakes into ganache. Top hazelnut cupcakes with reserved ground hazelnuts, top chocolate chip cupcakes with mini chocolate chips and top orange cupcakes with orange peel. Refrigerate at least 10 minutes before serving.

1 Cupcake: Calories 200 (Calories from Fat 100); Total Fat 11g (Saturated Fat 4g); Cholesterol 30mg; Sodium 180mg; Total Carbohydrate 24g (Dietary Fiber 1g)

*To toast hazelnuts, bake uncovered in ungreased shallow pan in a 350°F oven 6 to 10 minutes, stirring occasionally, until light brown. Rub the nuts with a towel to remove skins. Place nuts in food processor or blender; cover and process until ground.

4

holiday cupcakes

Heart Brownie Cupcakes

Prep Time: 30 min ▪ Start to Finish: 1 hr 30 min ▪ 24 Cupcakes

1 box (1 lb 6.5 oz) supreme brownie mix with pouch of chocolate flavor syrup
Water, vegetable oil and eggs called for on brownie mix box
1 to 2 tablespoons powdered sugar

1 Heat oven to 350°F. Place paper baking cup in each of 24 regular-size muffin cups. Spray cups with cooking spray. Make brownie batter as directed using water, oil and eggs. Fill each baking cup with 2 level measuring tablespoons batter.

2 Bake 24 to 26 minutes or until toothpick inserted in center comes out almost clean. Cool in pan 20 minutes. Carefully remove paper baking cups from muffins; cool upside down about 15 minutes or until completely cool.

3 Cut small heart out of paper. Place on bottom of cupcake. Sprinkle with powdered sugar. Carefully remove heart. Repeat with remaining cupcakes.

1 Cupcake: Calories 140 (Calories from Fat 40); Total Fat 5g (Saturated Fat 1g); Cholesterol 20mg; Sodium 95mg; Total Carbohydrate 23g (Dietary Fiber 0g)

Chocolate Truffle Brownie Cups

Prep Time: 15 min   Start to Finish: 1 hr 35 min   48 Brownie cups

1 box (1 lb 2.3 oz) fudge brownie mix
1/4 cup water
1/2 cup vegetable oil
2 eggs
2/3 cup whipping cream
6 oz semisweet baking chocolate, chopped
Chocolate sprinkles, if desired

1 Heat oven to 350°F. Place mini paper baking cup in each of 48 mini muffin pan cups OR use mini foil muffin cups if you don't have mini muffin pans. In large bowl, stir brownie mix, water, oil and eggs until well blended. Divide batter evenly among muffin cups.

2 Bake 20 to 22 minutes or until toothpick inserted into edge of muffin comes out clean. Cool 10 minutes before removing from pan. Cool completely, about 30 minutes.

3 Heat whipping cream in 1-quart saucepan over low heat just until hot but not boiling; remove from heat. Stir in chocolate until melted. Let stand about 15 minutes or until mixture coats spoon. (It will become firmer the longer it cools.) Spoon about 2 teaspoons chocolate mixture over each brownie. Sprinkle with chocolate sprinkles.

1 Brownie Cup: Calories 80 (Calories from Fat 45); Total Fat 5g (Saturated Fat 2g); Cholesterol 15mg; Sodium 5mg; Total Carbohydrate 9g (Dietary Fiber 1g)

Triple-Chocolate Mini Cups

Prep Time: 1 hr 25 min ▮ Start to Finish: 2 hr 25 min ▮ 72 Mini cups

3/4 cup butter or margarine

4 oz unsweetened baking chocolate

2 cups sugar

1 1/2 cups all-purpose flour

1/2 cup baking cocoa

2 teaspoons baking powder

1/2 teaspoon salt

4 eggs

1 1/2 cups semisweet chocolate chips

72 whole candied cherries, pecan halves, chocolate chunks or milk chocolate candy drops

1 Heat oven to 350°F. Place mini paper baking cups in mini muffin pan cups OR use mini foil muffin cups if you don't have mini muffin pans.

2 In 2-quart saucepan, melt butter and chocolate over low heat 6 to 10 minutes, stirring occasionally, until smooth; cool 20 minutes. In large bowl, beat melted chocolate mixture, sugar, 1 cup of the flour, the cocoa, baking powder, salt and eggs with electric mixer on medium speed about 2 minutes, scraping bowl occasionally, until well blended. Stir in remaining 1/2 cup flour and the chocolate chips. Drop dough by rounded teaspoons into mini cups.

3 Bake 15 to 17 minutes or until edges are slightly firm (center will be slightly soft). Immediately top each with cherry, pecan half or chocolate, pressing slightly. Cool completely, about 1 hour.

1 Mini Cup: Calories 80 (Calories from Fat 40); Total Fat 4g (Saturated Fat 2g); Cholesterol 15mg; Sodium 50mg; Total Carbohydrate 11g (Dietary Fiber 0g)

Top these gems with an assortment of cherries, pecans and chocolate and you'll have a variety to give as gifts.

Chirping Chick Cupcakes

Prep Time: 30 min ■ Start to Finish: 1 hr 45 min ■ 24 Cupcakes

1 box (1 lb 2.25 oz) yellow or white cake mix with pudding in the mix
Water, vegetable oil and eggs called for on cake mix box
2 containers (12 oz each) fluffy white whipped ready-to-spread frosting
Yellow food color
24 orange jelly beans
48 small orange candies

1 Heat oven to 350°F. Make and bake cake as directed on box for 24 cupcakes, using water, oil and eggs. Cool in pan 10 minutes; remove from pan to cooling rack. Cool completely, about 30 minutes.

2 Frost cupcakes with 1 container of frosting.

3 Stir a few drops yellow food color into other container of frosting. Spoon 1 heaping teaspoonful yellow frosting on center of each cupcake. To make beak, cut orange jelly bean lengthwise to within ⅛ inch of end; spread apart slightly. Press into yellow frosting. Add orange candies for eyes. Store loosely covered.

1 Cupcake (Cake and Frosting): Calories 270 (Calories from Fat 100); Total Fat 11g (Saturated Fat 3g); Cholesterol 25mg; Sodium 180mg; Total Carbohydrate 41g (Dietary Fiber 0g)

Hopping Bunny Cupcakes

Prep Time: 30 min ▪ Start to Finish: 1 hr 45 min ▪ 24 Cupcakes

1 box (1 lb 2.25 oz) yellow or white cake mix with pudding in the mix
Water, vegetable oil and eggs called for on cake mix box
Few drops red food color
2 containers (12 oz each) fluffy white whipped ready-to-spread frosting
5 large marshmallows
Pink sugar
Candy decorations and sprinkles, as desired

1 Heat oven to 350°F. Make and bake cake mix as directed on box for 24 cupcakes, using water, oil and eggs. Cool 10 minutes; remove from pan to cooling rack. Cool completely, about 30 minutes.

2 Stir just enough red food color into 1 container of frosting to tint frosting pink. Frost cupcakes with pink frosting.

3 Spoon 1 heaping teaspoonful white frosting on center of each cupcake. To make ears, cut each large marshmallow crosswise into 5 pieces, using kitchen scissors. Using scissors, cut through center of each marshmallow piece to within ¼ inch of edge. Separate to look like bunny ears; press 1 side of cut edges into pink sugar, flattening slightly. Arrange on each of the white frosting mounds. Use candy decorations and sprinkles to make eyes, nose and whiskers. Store loosely covered.

1 Cupcake (Cake and Frosting): Calories 250 (Calories from Fat 100); Total Fat 11g (Saturated Fat 3g); Cholesterol 25mg; Sodium 180mg; Total Carbohydrate 35g (Dietary Fiber 0g)

Stars and Stripes Cupcakes

Prep Time: 45 min ▪ Start to Finish: 1 hr 45 min ▪ 8 Cupcakes

Cupcakes
3/4 cup all-purpose flour
3/4 teaspoon baking powder
1/4 teaspoon salt
1/4 cup butter or margarine, softened
1/3 cup granulated sugar
1/2 cup sour cream
2 eggs
1/2 teaspoon almond extract

1 jar (6 oz) maraschino cherries (about 16 cherries), drained, finely chopped and patted dry

Glaze and Decoration
1 cup powdered sugar
1 tablespoon light corn syrup
2 teaspoons water
1/4 teaspoon almond extract
1 tube (4.25 oz) red decorating icing
8 blue candy stars

1 Heat oven to 350°F. Place red paper baking cup in each of 8 regular-size muffin cups. In small bowl, mix flour, baking powder and salt; set aside.

2 In medium bowl, beat butter and granulated sugar with electric mixer on high speed until creamy. Add sour cream, eggs and ½ teaspoon almond extract; beat until well blended. On low speed, beat in flour mixture just until blended. Stir in cherries. Divide batter evenly among muffin cups.

3 Bake 20 to 25 minutes or until toothpick inserted in center comes out clean. Cool 5 minutes; remove to cooling rack. Cool completely, about 30 minutes.

4 Meanwhile, in small bowl, stir together powdered sugar, corn syrup, water and ¼ teaspoon almond extract. Spoon over cupcakes, using back of spoon to spread. Let stand 10 minutes.

5 Place tube of red icing in 4-cup measuring cup filled with warm water; let stand 5 minutes. Meanwhile, place 1 blue candy star on each cupcake about ¼ inch from edge. Remove tube of red icing from water; wipe dry. Squeeze tube several times to mix and soften icing. Using red icing with writing tip, pipe wavy stripes on cupcakes to resemble flag with star in the upper left corner.

1 Cupcake: Calories 270 (Calories from Fat 90); Total Fat 11g (Saturated Fat 6g); Cholesterol 80mg; Sodium 190mg; Total Carbohydrate 41g (Dietary Fiber 0g)

Star-Studded Cupcakes

Prep Time: 25 min ▮ Start to Finish: 1 hr 20 min ▮ 36 Cupcakes

4 oz semisweet or white chocolate baking bar, melted
White chocolate baking bar, melted, if desired
2 cups all-purpose flour
2 cups sugar
1 1/4 teaspoons baking soda
1 teaspoon salt
1/2 teaspoon baking powder
1 cup water

3/4 cup sour cream
1/4 cup shortening
1 teaspoon vanilla
2 eggs
4 oz unsweetened baking chocolate, melted, cooled
1 container (1 lb) chocolate creamy or creamy white ready-to-spread frosting

1 In 1-quart saucepan, melt chocolate over low heat, stirring frequently. Place waxed paper on cookie sheet. Spread melted chocolate in 8-inch square on waxed paper. Refrigerate until firm, about 1 hour.

2 Remove chocolate from refrigerator; let stand until room temperature. Cut with cookie cutters of desired shapes and sizes. Refrigerate until ready to place on cupcakes. Carefully peel cutouts from waxed paper, handling as little as possible. Dip half of each cutout into melted white baking chocolate; refrigerate until set.

3 Heat oven to 350°F. Place paper baking cup in each of 36 regular-size muffin cups. In large bowl, beat all remaining ingredients except frosting with electric mixer on low speed 30 seconds, scraping bowl constantly. Beat on high speed 3 minutes, scraping bowl constantly. Divide batter evenly among muffin cups.

4 Bake 20 to 25 minutes or until toothpick inserted in center comes out clean. Remove from pan to cooling rack. Cool completely, about 30 minutes.

5 Frost cupcakes. Garnish with chocolate cutouts.

1 Cupcake: Calories 165 (Calories from Fat 55); Total Fat 6g (Saturated Fat 4g); Cholesterol 15mg; Sodium 120mg; Total Carbohydrate 27g (Dietary Fiber 1g)

Black Cat Cupcakes

Prep Time: 30 min ▪ Start to Finish: 1 hr 45 min ▪ 24 Cupcakes

Chocolate Cupcakes (page 141)
Creamy Chocolate Frosting (page 148)
12 thin chocolate wafer cookies, cut into 4 wedges
48 red miniature jelly beans
24 blackberry nonpareil-covered chewy candies
Black string licorice

1 Bake Chocolate Cupcakes as directed for muffin cups to make 24 cupcakes. Make Creamy Chocolate Frosting; frost cupcakes.

2 For ears for each cupcake, add 2 wafer cookie wedges. Add red jelly beans for eyes and blackberry candy for nose. Add pieces of licorice for whiskers.

1 Cupcake (Cake and Frosting): Calories 310 (Calories from Fat 130); Total Fat 14g (Saturated Fat 6g); Cholesterol 30mg; Sodium 210mg; Total Carbohydrate 43g (Dietary Fiber 2g)

Make Gumdrop Black Cat Cupcakes. Here's how: Bake cupcakes as directed. Make Creamy White Frosting (page 149); tint with 6 drops each red and yellow food colors to make orange. Frost cupcakes. For each gumdrop cat, cut a large black gumdrop crosswise into 3 pieces. Use small rounded top piece for head and largest bottom piece for body. Cut tail and ears from middle piece. Arrange on frosting to form cat.

Ghost Cupcakes,
page 100

Black Cat
Cupcakes

Witches Cupcakes,
page 101

Ghost Cupcakes

Prep Time: 35 min ▮ Start to Finish: 1 hr 50 min ▮ 24 Cupcakes

White Cupcakes (page 144)
Creamy White Frosting (page 149)
48 large marshmallows
Toothpicks
48 miniature chocolate chips
12 orange jelly beans, cut in half

1 Bake White Cupcakes as directed for muffin cups to make 24 cupcakes. Make Creamy White Frosting; frost cupcakes, reserving some frosting for attaching ghosts.

2 For each ghost, attach 2 marshmallows with toothpick. Add chocolate chips for eyes and jelly bean half for mouth, using small amount of frosting.

3 Place ghost on each cupcake, bringing frosting up around bottom so ghost appears to be coming from frosting. Dab a small amount of frosting on top of each ghost.

1 Cupcake (Cake and Frosting): Calories 380 (Calories from Fat 120); Total Fat 13g (Saturated Fat 3.5g); Cholesterol 0mg; Sodium 190mg; Total Carbohydrate 64g (Dietary Fiber 0g)

Photo, page 99.

Witches Cupcakes

Prep Time: 30 min ■ Start to Finish: 1 hr 45 min ■ 24 Cupcakes

1 box (1 lb 2.25 oz) yellow cake mix with pudding in the mix
Water, vegetable oil and eggs called for on cake mix box
1 container (1 lb) vanilla creamy frosting
Green paste food color
Black licorice twists
Candy corn
Yellow candy-coated peanut butter or chocolate candies
1 tube (0.68 oz) black decorating gel

1 Heat oven to 350°F. Place paper baking cup in each of 24 regular-size muffin cups. Make cake mix as directed on box, using water, oil and eggs. Divide batter evenly among muffin cups.

2 Bake 18 to 23 minutes or until toothpick inserted in center comes out clean. Immediately remove from pan to cooling rack. Cool completely, about 1 hour.

3 Tint frosting with food color. Cut licorice twists into various lengths. Frost cupcakes with frosting. Arrange licorice pieces on each cupcake for hat. Add candy corn for nose and peanut butter candies for eyes. Make pupils of eyes and the mouth with decorating gel.

1 Cupcake (Cake and Frosting): Calories 210 (Calories from Fat 90); Total Fat 10g (Saturated Fat 3g); Cholesterol 25mg; Sodium 190mg; Total Carbohydrate 28g (Dietary Fiber 0g)

Photo, page 99.

Spooky Kooky Cupcakes

Prep Time: 40 min ■ Start to Finish: 2 hr 10 min ■ 24 Cupcakes

1 box (1 lb 2.25 oz) devil's food cake mix with pudding in the mix
Water, vegetable oil and eggs called for on cake mix box
1 container (1 lb) creamy white ready-to-spread frosting
1 tube (0.68 oz) black decorating gel
1 cup assorted small candies (such as tiny jelly beans or candy corn)

1 Heat oven to 350°F. Make and bake cake as directed on box for 24 cupcakes, using water, oil and eggs. Cool in pan 10 minutes; remove from pan to cooling rack. Cool completely, about 30 minutes.

2 To decorate each cupcake, spoon about 1 tablespoonful frosting on top of each. With back of spoon, spread frosting into shape of light bulb to make skeleton head. While frosting is still wet, decorate with gel and candies to make skeleton face.

1 Cupcake: Calories 260 (Calories from Fat 100); Total Fat 11g (Saturated Fat 3.5g); Cholesterol 25mg; Sodium 230mg; Total Carbohydrate 38g (Dietary Fiber 0g)

Spiderweb Cupcakes

Prep Time: 20 min ▪ Start to Finish: 1 hr 25 min ▪ 24 Cupcakes

1 box (1 lb 2.25 oz) devil's food cake
 mix with pudding in the mix
Water, vegetable oil and eggs called
 for on cake mix box
1 container (1 lb) vanilla creamy ready-
 to-spread frosting or Vanilla
 Buttercream Frosting (page 146)

3 drops red food color
4 or 5 drops yellow food color
1 tube (0.68 oz) black or white
 decorating gel
48 large black gumdrops

1 Heat oven to 350°F. Grease bottoms only of 24 regular-size muffin cups or line with paper baking cups. Make and bake cake as directed on box for 24 cupcakes, using water, oil and eggs. Divide batter evenly among muffin cups.

2 Bake 18 to 23 minutes or until toothpick inserted in center comes out clean. Cool 10 minutes; remove from pan to cooling rack. Cool completely, about 30 minutes.

3 Tint frosting with red and yellow food colors to make orange frosting. Spread frosting over tops of cupcakes.

4 Squeeze circles of decorating gel on each cupcake; pull knife through gel from center outward to make web. To make each spider, roll out 1 gumdrop and cut out 8 strips for legs; place another gumdrop on top. Place spider on cupcake. Store loosely covered at room temperature.

1 Cupcake: Calories 265 (Calories from Fat 70); Total Fat 8g (Saturated Fat 3g); Cholesterol 15mg; Sodium 130mg; Total Carbohydrate 47g (Dietary Fiber 0g)

Get the kids to help! Kids can make spider legs without cutting gumdrops by pinching and gently rolling gumdrops back and forth between their fingertips into long thin strips. The more they roll them, the stickier the gumdrops will become. Have the kids dip rolled gumdrops in sugar as needed to make them less sticky.

Scarecrow and Spider Cupcakes

Prep Time: 30 min ▪ Start to Finish: 50 min ▪ 16 Cupcakes

1½ cups Original Bisquick mix
½ cup sugar
½ cup milk or water
2 tablespoons shortening
1 tablespoon vanilla
1 egg
1 container (1 lb) vanilla or butter cream creamy ready-to-spread frosting
8 fudge-dipped flat-bottom ice cream cones
Strawberry chewy fruit snack in 3-foot rolls

Shredded whole wheat cereal biscuits, crushed
Assorted candies, such as candy corn, red string licorice and small gumdrops
32 candy eyes
1 container (1 lb) chocolate creamy ready-to-spread frosting
48 large black gumdrops
Black string licorice, cut into 4-inch pieces

1 Heat oven to 375°F. Place paper baking cup in each of 16 regular-size muffin cups, or grease and flour muffin cups.

2 In large bowl, beat Bisquick mix, sugar, milk, shortening, vanilla and egg with electric mixer on low speed 30 seconds, scraping bowl constantly. Beat on medium speed 4 minutes, scraping bowl occasionally. Divide batter evenly among muffin cups.

3 Bake 15 to 20 minutes or until toothpick inserted in center comes out clean. Immediately remove from pan; cool completely.

4 For scarecrows, frost 8 cupcakes with vanilla frosting. Decorate each ice-cream cone with bow made with fruit rolls. Place ice cream cone upside down on each cupcake for hat. Arrange crushed cereal on cupcakes for hair. Use candy corn for nose, red licorice and small gumdrops for mouth and candy eyes for eyes.

5 For hairy spiders frost 8 cupcakes with chocolate frosting. Squeeze 44 large black gumdrops, one at a time, through garlic press to form hair; arrange on cupcakes. Cut remaining large black gumdrops in half. Insert black

licorice pieces into cupcakes for legs. Place candy eyes on halved large black gumdrops for head.

1 Serving: Calories 350 (Calories from Fat 100); Total Fat 11g (Saturated Fat 7g); Cholesterol 15mg; Sodium 190mg; Total Carbohydrate 66g (Dietary Fiber 1g)

Black string licorice is easier to work with when it's slightly warm. Soften in the microwave on Medium for 5 to 10 seconds.

Autumn Leaf Cupcakes

Prep Time: 45 min ■ Start to Finish: 1 hr 30 min ■ 24 Cupcakes

1 box (1 lb 2.25 oz) devil's food cake mix with pudding in the mix
Water, vegetable oil and eggs called for on cake mix box
1/2 cup semisweet chocolate chips, melted
1/2 cup butterscotch chips, melted
1 container (1 lb) chocolate creamy ready-to-spread frosting

1 Heat oven to 350°F. Make and bake cake mix as directed on box for 24 cupcakes, using water, oil and eggs. Cool 10 minutes; remove from pan to cooling racks. Cool completely, about 30 minutes.

2 Meanwhile, place 12-inch sheet of waxed paper on cookie sheet; mark an 8-inch square on waxed paper. Alternately place spoonfuls of melted chocolate and butterscotch on waxed paper. With small spatula, swirl together for marbled effect, spreading to an 8-inch square. Refrigerate until firm, about 30 minutes.

3 Remove from refrigerator; let stand about 10 minutes or until slightly softened. Use 1½-inch leaf cookie cutter to make 24 leaf cutouts. Carefully remove cutouts from paper with spatula; place on another waxed paper–lined cookie sheet. Refrigerate until firm, about 5 minutes.

4 Frost cupcakes. Garnish with leaf cutouts. Store loosely covered in refrigerator.

1 Cupcake: Calories 250 (Calories from Fat 120); Total Fat 13g (Saturated Fat 4g); Cholesterol 25mg; Sodium 240mg; Total Carbohydrate 32g (Dietary Fiber 0g)

Thanksgiving Turkey Cupcakes

Prep Time: 45 min ■ Start to Finish: 2 hr ■ 24 Cupcakes

1 box (1 lb 2.25 oz) yellow cake mix with pudding in the mix	1 container (1 lb) chocolate creamy ready-to-spread frosting
1¼ cups water	4 oz vanilla-flavored candy coating (almond bark)
¼ cup vegetable oil	4 oz semisweet baking chocolate
3 eggs	24 Kisses® milk chocolates, unwrapped
¾ cup creamy peanut butter	

1 Heat oven to 350°F. Place paper baking cup in each of 24 regular-size muffin cups.

2 In large bowl, beat cake mix, water, oil, eggs and peanut butter with electric mixer on low speed 30 seconds. Beat on medium speed 2 minutes, scraping bowl occasionally. Divide batter evenly among muffin cups.

3 Bake 20 to 25 minutes or until toothpick inserted in center comes out clean. Remove cupcakes from pan to cooling rack. Cool completely, about 30 minutes. Frost cupcakes with frosting.

4 Line cookie sheet with waxed paper. In separate small microwavable bowls, microwave candy coating and baking chocolate uncovered on High 30 to 60 seconds, stirring every 15 seconds, until melted and smooth. Place coating and chocolate in separate resealable food-storage plastic bags; snip off tiny corner of each bag. Pipe coating and chocolate into fan shapes to resemble turkey tail feathers. Refrigerate coating and chocolate about 5 minutes until set.

5 When set, peel feathers off waxed paper and insert into cupcakes. Place milk chocolate candy on each cupcake for head of turkey.

1 Cupcake: Calories 320 (Calories from Fat 150): Total Fat 17g (Saturated Fat 6g): Cholesterol 30mg; Sodium 250mg; Total Carbohydrate 38g (Dietary Fiber 0g)

Hershey®'s Kisses®, the Conical Configuration and Plume Device are registered trademarks of Hershey Foods Corporation

Holly-Day Red Velvet Cupcakes

Prep Time: 40 min ▪ Start to Finish: 1 hr 30 min ▪ 24 Cupcakes

Cupcakes
2¼ cups all-purpose flour
¼ cup unsweetened baking cocoa
1 teaspoon salt
½ cup butter or margarine, softened
1½ cups granulated sugar
2 eggs
1 bottle (1 oz) red food color
1½ teaspoons vanilla

1 cup buttermilk
1 teaspoon baking soda
1 tablespoon white vinegar
Marshmallow Buttercream Frosting
1 jar (7 oz) marshmallow creme
1 cup butter or margarine, softened
2 cups powdered sugar
24 spearmint gumdrop leaves
72 red cinnamon candies

1 Heat oven to 350°F. Place paper baking cup in each of 24 regular-size muffin cups. In small bowl, mix flour, cocoa and salt; set aside. In large bowl, beat ½ cup butter and granulated sugar with electric mixer on medium speed until mixed. Add eggs; beat 1 to 2 minutes or until light and fluffy. Stir in food color and vanilla.

2 Beat in flour mixture alternately with buttermilk on low speed just until blended. Beat in baking soda and vinegar until well blended. Divide batter evenly among muffin cups.

3 Bake 20 to 22 minutes or until toothpick inserted in center comes out clean. Remove to cooling racks. Cool completely, about 30 minutes.

4 Remove lid and foil seal from jar of marshmallow creme. Microwave on High 15 to 20 seconds to soften. In large bowl, beat marshmallow creme and 1 cup butter with electric mixer on medium speed until smooth. Beat in powdered sugar until smooth.

5 Spoon 1 heaping tablespoon frosting onto each cupcake, swirling frosting with back of spoon. Cut one spearmint leaf candy in half horizontally; place leaves on frosting, pressing down slightly to form holly sprig. Place 3 red cinnamon candies in center of sprig, pressing down slightly, for berries.

1 Cupcake: Calories 280 (Calories from Fat 110); Total Fat 12g (Saturated Fat 6g); Cholesterol 50mg; Sodium 250mg; Total Carbohydrate 39g (Dietary Fiber 0g)

Reindeer Cupcakes

Prep Time: 20 min ▪ Start to Finish: 1 hr 20 min ▪ 24 Cupcakes

1 box (1 lb 2.25 oz) cake mix with pudding in the mix (any flavor)
Water, vegetable oil and eggs called for on cake mix box
1 container (1 lb) chocolate creamy ready-to-spread frosting
Chocolate sprinkles
24 large pretzel twists
24 mini marshmallows
24 small green gumdrops
24 red cinnamon candies

1 Heat oven to 350°F. Make and bake cake mix as directed on package for 24 cupcakes, using water, oil and eggs. Cool in pan 10 minutes; remove from pan to cooling rack. Cool completely, about 30 minutes.

2 Frost cupcakes with frosting. Sprinkle with chocolate sprinkles. For each cupcake, break pretzel twist in half; arrange on cupcake for antlers.

3 Cut marshmallow in half; arrange on cupcake for eyes. Place gumdrop on cupcake for nose. Place red cinnamon candy below gumdrop for mouth. Store loosely covered at room temperature.

1 Cupcake (Cake and Frosting): Calories 270 (Calories from Fat 90); Total Fat 10g (Saturated Fat 2¹/₂g); Cholesterol 25mg; Sodium 310mg; Total Carbohydrate 43g (Dietary Fiber 0g)

Snowman Cupcakes

Prep Time: 45 min ▪ Start to Finish: 2 hr ▪ 24 Cupcakes

White Cupcakes (page 144)
Creamy Vanilla Frosting (page 148)
White edible glitter or decorator sugar crystals
1 bag (16 oz) large marshmallows
Pretzel sticks
Chewy fruit snack in 3-foot rolls, any red or orange flavor (from 4.5-oz box)
Assorted candies (such as gumdrops, gummy ring candies, peppermint candies,
    chocolate chips, pastel mint chips, candy decors, string licorice)

1 Bake White Cupcakes as directed for muffin cups to make 24 cupcakes. Make Creamy Vanilla Frosting; frost cupcakes. Sprinkle frosting with edible glitter.

2 Stack 2 or 3 marshmallows on each cupcake, using ½ teaspoon frosting between marshmallows to attach.

3 For arms, break pretzel sticks into pieces 1½ inches long. Press 2 pieces into marshmallow on each cupcake. Cut 1-inch mitten shapes from fruit snack. Attach mittens to pretzels.

4 For scarf, cut fruit snack into 6 × ¼-inch piece; wrap and tie around base of top marshmallow. For hat, stack candies, using frosting to attach. For earmuff, use piece of string licorice and candies, using frosting to attach.

5 For faces and buttons, attach desired candies with small amount of frosting.

1 Cupcake (Cake and Frosting): Calories 390 (Calories from Fat 100); Total Fat 11g (Saturated Fat 4g); Cholesterol 15mg; Sodium 230mg; Total Carbohydrate 69g (Dietary Fiber 0g)

Make your own snow creatures!

There are lots of clever ways that snow people can be decorated; check your pantry for colorful candies you might have on hand.

Cupcake Pet Parade

Prep Time: 45 min ▪ Start to Finish: 2 hr ▪ 24 Cupcakes

White Cupcakes (page 144)
1 container (1 lb) vanilla creamy ready-to-spread frosting
1 tablespoon chocolate-flavored syrup
Chewy fruit snack in 3-foot rolls, any flavor (from 4.5-oz box)
24 semisweet chocolate chips
16 large white gumdrops
1 tube (0.68 oz) pink decorating gel
24 miniature candy-coated chocolate baking bits
8 miniature creme-filled chocolate sandwich cookies
1 tube (0.68 oz) black decorating gel
Small gumdrops

1 Make White Cupcakes as directed for 24 muffin cups to make cupcakes.

2 For cats, stir together ½ cup of the frosting and the chocolate syrup. Spread chocolate frosting over tops of 8 cupcakes. Cut small pieces of fruit snack for ears. Cut additional fruit snack into 1 × ¼-inch strips for whiskers. Use chocolate chips for nose and eyes. Arrange on frosting to make cat faces.

3 For rabbits, spread half of the remaining vanilla frosting over tops of 8 cupcakes. Flatten large white gumdrops with rolling pin; slightly fold and shape to form ears. Use pink gel to make inner ears. Cut fruit snack or flatten gumdrops and cut into 2¼-inch strips for whiskers. Use baking bits for eyes and nose. Arrange on frosting to make rabbit faces.

4 For dogs, spread remaining vanilla frosting over tops of remaining 8 cupcakes. Break or cut cookies in half; press 2 halves in each frosted cupcake for ears. Use black gel for spots or streaks on face. Use pieces of gumdrops for eyes and nose. Flatten additional gumdrops for tongue. Arrange on frosting to make dog faces.

1 Cupcake (Cake and Frosting): Calories 250 (Calories from Fat 100); Total Fat 11g (Saturated Fat 3.5g); Cholesterol 0mg; Sodium 240mg; Total Carbohydrate 35g (Dietary Fiber 0g)

Teddy Bear Cupcakes

Prep Time: 35 min ▪ Start to Finish: 1 hr 45 min ▪ 24 Cupcakes

1 box (1 lb 2.25 oz) yellow cake mix
    with pudding in the mix
1 cup water
1/2 cup creamy peanut butter
3 eggs
1 container (12 oz) chocolate whipped
    ready-to-spread frosting

1/3 cup miniature semisweet
    chocolate chips
1/3 cup honey-flavor dry-roasted
    peanuts, chopped
48 teddy bear–shaped graham
    snacks
24 birthday candles

1 Heat oven to 350°F. Place paper baking cup in each of 24 regular-size muffin cups.

2 In large bowl, beat cake mix, water, peanut butter and eggs with electric mixer on low speed 30 seconds. Beat on medium speed 1 minute, scraping bowl occasionally. Divide batter evenly among muffin cups.

3 Bake 13 to 18 minutes or until toothpick inserted in center comes out clean and tops spring back when touched lightly in center. Cool 10 minutes; remove from pan to cooling rack. Cool completely, about 30 minutes.

4 Reserve ¼ cup of the frosting. Spread remaining frosting over tops of cupcakes. Sprinkle each cupcake with ½ teaspoon each chocolate chips and peanuts; press gently into frosting.

5 Spread about ½ teaspoon reserved frosting on flat sides of 2 graham snacks. Place candle between frosted sides of graham snacks; press gently together. Repeat with remaining snacks, frosting and candles. Place on cupcakes, pressing slightly to hold in place. Store loosely covered at room temperature.

1 Cupcake: Calories 245 (Calories from Fat 110); Total Fat 12g (Saturated Fat 6g); Cholesterol 25mg; Sodium 200mg; Total Carbohydrate 30g (Dietary Fiber 1g)

Clown Cupcakes

Prep Time: 30 min ▪ Start to Finish: 1 hr 45 min ▪ 24 cupcakes

Yellow Cupcakes (page 145)
Creamy Vanilla Frosting (page 148)
Assorted candies (such as candy-coated fruit-flavored chewy candies and
    miniature candy-coated chocolate baking bits)
Candy-coated wafers
Nonpareil decors
1 tube (4.25 oz) red decorating icing

1 Bake Yellow Cupcakes as directed for muffin cups to make 24 cupcakes. Make Creamy Vanilla Frosting; frost cupcakes.

2 Use desired candies for eyes and nose. Add candy-coated wafers for ears. Sprinkle with nonpareil decors for hair. Pipe on mouth with decorating icing.

1 Cupcake (Cake and Frosting): Calories 300 (Calories from Fat 90); Total Fat 10g (Saturated Fat 5g); Cholesterol 50mg; Sodium 240mg; Total Carbohydrate 50g (Dietary Fiber 0g)

Add hats to your clown cupcakes:

Place sugar-style ice cream cone, pointed end up, on top and edge of frosted cupcake. For eyes and eyebrows, attach candies with small amount of frosting to cone. Decorate remaining clown face and hat as desired.

Lion Cupcakes

Prep Time: 30 min ▪ Start to Finish: 1 hr 45 min ▪ 24 Cupcakes

Yellow Cupcakes (page 145)

Creamy Vanilla Frosting (page 148) or Creamy Chocolate Frosting (page 148)

Yellow paste or gel icing color

Assorted candies (such as candy-coated chocolate candies, pastel-colored mint candy drops, gumdrops, jelly beans)

1 tube (4.25 oz) chocolate or white decorating icing

3 cups chow mein noodles

1 Bake Yellow Cupcakes as directed for muffin cups to make 24 cupcakes. Make Creamy Vanilla Frosting; tint with food color to make yellow. (Or make Creamy Chocolate Frosting.) Frost cupcakes.

2 Add candies for ears, eyes and muzzles. Pipe on whiskers with decorating icing. Add noodles along edge of each cupcake for mane.

1 Cupcake (Cake and Frosting): Calories 330 (Calories from Fat 90); Total Fat 10g (Saturated Fat 5g); Cholesterol 50mg; Sodium 250mg; Total Carbohydrate 57g (Dietary Fiber 0g)

Baseball Caps

Prep Time: 20 min ▮ Start to Finish: 1 hr 40 min ▮ 24 Cupcakes

> 1 box (1 lb 2.25 oz) yellow cake mix with pudding in the mix
> Water, vegetable oil and eggs called for on cake mix box
> 3 containers (1 lb each) vanilla ready-to-spread frosting
> Assorted food colors
> Black string licorice
> Assorted candy-coated fruit-flavored chewy candies
> Assorted fruit slice candies
> 1 tube (0.68 oz) decorating gel, if desired

1 Heat oven to 350°F. Place paper baking cup in each of 24 regular-size muffin cups. Make, bake and cool cake as directed on box for 24 cupcakes. Remove paper baking cups.

2 Divide frosting among small bowls for as many colors as desired; stir food color into each. Cut slice from top of each cupcake to make a flat surface. Turn cupcakes upside down. Frost top (formerly bottom) and sides of cupcakes.

3 Starting at center of each cap, place pieces of licorice down sides for seams. Place 1 candy-coated fruit candy at center top. Use fruit slices for brims (trim fruit slices if necessary). Pipe team initial or child's name on caps with decorating gel. Store loosely covered at room temperature.

1 Cupcake (Cake and Frosting): Calories 380 (Calories from Fat 160); Total Fat 17g (Saturated Fat 5g); Cholesterol 25mg; Sodium 290mg; Total Carbohydrate 54g (Dietary Fiber 0g)

Ball Game Cupcakes

Prep Time: 35 min ▪ Start to Finish: 1 hr 55 min ▪ 24 Cupcakes

1 box (1 lb 2.25 oz) yellow cake mix with pudding in the mix	1 container (1 lb) creamy white ready-to-spread frosting
Water, vegetable oil and eggs called for on cake mix box	Assorted colors decorating icing (in 4.25-oz tubes)
1 cup mini semisweet chocolate chips	Assorted food colors

1 Heat oven to 375°F. Place paper baking cup in each of 24 regular-size muffin cups. In large bowl, beat cake mix, water, oil and eggs with electric mixer on low speed 30 seconds. Beat on medium speed 2 minutes, scraping bowl occasionally. Fold in chocolate chips. Divide batter evenly among muffin cups.

2 Bake 20 to 25 minutes or until toothpick inserted in center comes out clean. Cool 10 minutes; remove to wire rack. Cool, about 30 minutes.

3 For Soccer Balls, frost cupcakes with vanilla frosting. With black icing, pipe a pentagon shape in the center of cupcake, piping a few rows of frosting into center of pentagon. Using a toothpick, trace a line from each point of pentagon to edge of cupcake to look like seams. With toothpick or spatula, spread black icing in center of pentagon to fill in the entire shape.

4 For Baseballs, frost cupcakes with vanilla frosting. With black, red or blue icing, pipe 2 arches on opposite sides of cupcakes, curving lines slightly toward center. Pipe small lines from each arch to look like stitches on a baseball.

5 For Basketballs, tint frosting with yellow and red food color to make orange. Frost cupcakes. With black icing, pipe line across center of cupcake. On either side, pipe an arch that curves slightly toward center line, then pipe a short line from center of each arch to edge of cupcake.

6 For Tennis Balls, tint frosting with yellow and green food color to make tennis-ball yellow. Frost cupcakes. With white icing, pipe curved design to look like tennis balls.

1 Cupcake: Calories 250 (Calories from Fat 110); Total Fat 12g (Saturated Fat 4g); Cholesterol 25mg; Sodium 200mg; Total Carbohydrate 33g (Dietary Fiber 0g)

Arrange cupcakes on green "grass."

To make grass, shake 1 cup coconut and 3 drops green food color in tightly covered jar or food-storage plastic bag until evenly tinted.

Goin' Fishin' Cupcakes

Prep Time: 35 min ‖ Start to Finish: 1 hr 35 min ‖ 24 Cupcakes

> 1 box (1 lb 2.25 oz) devil's food cake mix with pudding in the mix
> Water, vegetable oil and eggs called for on cake mix box
> 1 container (1 lb) vanilla creamy ready-to-spread frosting
> Blue liquid or paste food color
> 24 cocktail straws
> 24 pieces thick craft thread, dental floss or fish line, each 6½ inches long
> 24 assorted chewy fruit flavored snacks in shark shapes (from 2 to 3.9-oz packets)

1 Heat oven to 350°F. Place paper baking cup in each of 24 regular-size muffin cups. Make cake mix as directed on box, using water, oil and eggs. Divide batter evenly among muffin cups.

2 Bake 15 to 20 minutes or until toothpick inserted in center comes out clean. Cool 10 minutes; remove from pan to cooling rack. Cool completely, about 30 minutes.

3 In medium bowl, mix frosting and a few drops of food color. Frost cupcakes with blue frosting. Pull up on frosting, using metal spatula, so frosting looks like waves.

4 Cut each straw to make one 3-inch piece. Insert piece of craft thread into one end of each straw piece to look like fishing line. Attach 1 shark snack to other end of craft thread. Stick end of straw into cupcake to hold fishing pole upright, and gently press shark snack into icing. Store loosely covered at room temperature.

1 Cupcake: Calories 230 (Calories from Fat 100); Total Fat 11g (Saturated Fat 3g); Cholesterol 25mg; Sodium 230mg; Total Carbohydrate 31g (Dietary Fiber 0g)

Picnic Pals

Prep Time: 1 hr ▮ Start to Finish: 2 hr 10 min ▮ 24 Cupcakes

1 box (1 lb 2.25 oz) cake mix with pudding in the mix (any flavor)
Water, vegetable oil and eggs called for on cake mix box
1 container (12 oz) fluffy white or vanilla whipped ready-to-spread frosting
Assorted gumdrops or small candies
Chewy fruit snacks in 3-foot rolls, any flavor (from 4.5-oz box)
1 tube (0.68 oz) black decorating gel

1 Heat oven to 350°F. Place paper baking cup in each of 24 regular-size muffin cups. Make and bake cake mix as directed on box for cupcakes, using water, oil and eggs. Cool 10 minutes; remove from pan to cooling rack. Cool completely, about 30 minutes.

2 Frost and decorate 1 cupcake at a time. Decorate with whole or cut-up gumdrops, small candies, cut-up or thinly rolled fruit snacks and decorating gel to look like ladybugs, bumblebees, butterflies, caterpillars and beetles. Store loosely covered at room temperature.

1 Cupcake (Cake and Frosting): Calories 190 (Calories from Fat 80): Total Fat 9g (Saturated Fat 2g): Cholesterol 25mg: Sodium 160mg: Total Carbohydrate 26g (Dietary Fiber 0g)

When cutting gumdrops, dip knife or kitchen scissors into water to keep from sticking.

Flower Power Cupcakes

Prep Time: 30 min | Start to Finish: 1 hr 30 min | 24 Cupcakes

1 box (1 lb 2.25 oz) white cake mix with pudding in the mix
Water, vegetable oil and egg whites called for on cake mix box
1 container (12 oz) fluffy white whipped ready-to-spread frosting or 1 container
  (1 lb) lemon or strawberry ready-to-spread frosting
Multicolored licorice twists
Candy sprinkles

1 Heat oven to 350°F. Place paper baking cup in each of 24 regular-size muffin cups. Make and bake cake mix as directed on box for 24 cupcakes, using water, oil and eggs. Cool 10 minutes; remove from pan to cooling rack. Cool completely, about 30 minutes.

2 Frost cupcakes with frosting.

3 Cut licorice into desired size pieces. Create flower shapes with licorice; arrange on cupcakes, using additional frosting to attach licorice. Sprinkle candy sprinkles in center of each flower.

1 Cupcake: Calories 180 (Calories from Fat 70); Total Fat 8g (Saturated Fat 2g); Cholesterol 0mg; Sodium 170mg; Total Carbohydrate 25g (Dietary Fiber 0g)

Frog Cupcakes

Prep Time: 30 min ▮ Start to Finish: 1 hr 45 min ▮ 24 Cupcakes

White Cupcakes (page 144)
Creamy Vanilla Frosting (page 148)
Green paste or gel icing color
48 green miniature vanilla wafer cookies
48 red cinnamon candies
1 tube (4.25 oz) red decorating icing
Large red gumdrops

1 Bake White Cupcakes as directed for muffin cups to make 24 cupcakes. Make Creamy Vanilla Frosting; reserve 2 tablespoons white frosting. Tint remaining frosting with icing color to make green; frost cupcakes.

2 For eyes, place 2 cookies near top edge of each cupcake, inserting on end so they stand up. Attach 1 cinnamon candy to each cookie with reserved white frosting. Add dots of white frosting for nostrils.

3 For mouth, pipe on red icing. Slice gumdrops; add slice to each cupcake for tongue.

1 Cupcake (Cake and Frosting): Calories 170 (Calories from Fat 50); Total Fat 6g (Saturated Fat 2.5g); Cholesterol 15mg; Sodium 50mg; Total Carbohydrate 30g (Dietary Fiber 0g)

Pull-Apart Turtle Cupcakes

Prep Time: 30 min ▪ Start to Finish: 2 hr ▪ 24 Cupcakes (2 turtles)

1 box (1 lb 2.25 oz) yellow cake mix with pudding in the mix
Water, vegetable oil and eggs called for on cake mix box
1 container (1 lb) vanilla creamy ready-to-spread frosting
Green food color

1 container (1 lb) chocolate creamy ready-to-spread frosting
1 can (6.4 oz) green decorating icing
4 candy-coated chocolate candies
1 piece red string licorice
1 piece green peelable string licorice
1 can (6.4 oz) black decorating icing

1 Heat oven to 375°F. Place paper baking cup in each of 24 regular-size muffin cups. In large bowl, beat cake mix, water, oil and eggs with electric mixer on low speed 30 seconds. Beat on medium speed 2 minutes, scraping bowl occasionally. Divide batter evenly among muffin cups.

2 Bake 17 to 20 minutes or until toothpick inserted in center comes out clean. Cool 10 minutes; remove from pan to cooling rack. Cool completely, about 30 minutes.

3 Tint vanilla frosting with green food color. Reserve ½ cup green frosting and ½ cup chocolate frosting.

4 On each of 2 large serving trays, arrange 12 cupcakes as shown in diagram. Frost shell of one turtle with remaining chocolate frosting. Frost head and feet with reserved ½ cup green frosting. (Push cupcakes together slightly to frost entire turtle, not just individual cupcakes.) Pipe canned green icing on chocolate shell to create turtle design. Add 2 candies for eyes, a piece of red string licorice for mouth and a piece of green peelable string licorice for tail.

5 Frost remaining cupcakes using remaining green frosting for shell and reserved chocolate frosting for head and feet. Pipe canned black icing on green shell to create turtle design. Add 2 candies for eyes, a piece of red string licorice for mouth and a piece of green peelable string licorice for tail. Store loosely covered at room temperature.

1 Cupcake: Calories 360 (Calories from Fat 150); Total Fat 17g (Saturated Fat 6g); Cholesterol 25mg; Sodium 270mg; Total Carbohydrate 50g (Dietary Fiber 0g)

Dirt and Worms Cupcakes

Prep Time: 20 min ▪ Start to Finish: 1 hr 10 min ▪ 24 Cupcakes

1 cup water	$^1/_2$ cup shortening
$^1/_2$ cup unsweetened baking cocoa	2 eggs
1 $^2/_3$ cups all-purpose flour	1 container (1 lb) chocolate creamy
1 $^1/_2$ cups sugar	ready-to-spread frosting
1 teaspoon baking soda	Chopped pecans, if desired
$^1/_2$ teaspoon baking powder	Assorted candy decorations, if desired
$^1/_2$ teaspoon salt	24 gummy worm candies

1 Heat oven to 400°F. Place paper baking cups in each of 24 regular-size muffin cups. In medium microwavable bowl, heat water on High 1 minute. Stir in cocoa with spoon until smooth. Cool 5 minutes.

2 With electric mixer, beat in flour, sugar, baking soda, baking powder, salt, shortening and eggs on low speed 2 minutes, scraping bowl constantly. Beat on medium speed 2 minutes, scraping bowl frequently. Divide batter evenly among muffin cups.

3 Bake 15 to 20 minutes or until toothpick inserted in center comes out clean. Cool completely, about 30 minutes.

4 Frost cupcakes with frosting. Sprinkle with pecans and candy decorations. Add gummy worms, gently pushing one end into cupcake.

1 Cupcake: Calories 240 (Calories from Fat 80); Total Fat 9g (Saturated Fat 2.5g); Cholesterol 20mg; Sodium 180mg; Total Carbohydrate 38g (Dietary Fiber 0g)

For a bake sale or a birthday bash, fill a new toy dump truck with cookie crumbs, gummy worms and decorated cupcakes.

Orange Soda Cupcake Cones

Prep Time: 25 min ▌ Start to Finish: 1 hr 50 min ▌ 18 Cupcake cones

18 flat-bottom ice cream cones
Batter from Orange Soda Cupcakes (page 143)
1 container (1 lb) vanilla creamy ready-to-spread frosting
¼ cup finely crushed orange-flavored hard candies
Additional finely crushed orange-flavored hard candies, if desired
9 striped candy sticks (5 inches long) or plastic straws

1 Heat oven to 350°F. Stand cones upright in regular-size muffin cups or 13 × 9-inch pan.

2 Make Orange Soda Cupcake batter as directed. Pour batter into cones, filling each to within about ¼ inch from top.

3 Bake 22 to 25 minutes or until toothpick inserted in center of cake comes out clean. Remove cones from muffin cups to cooling rack. Cool completely, about 1 hour.

4 In small bowl, mix frosting and ¼ cup crushed candies. Spread over tops of cone cupcakes. Sprinkle with additional candies. Cut or break candy sticks in half; insert into each frosted cupcake cone.

1 Cupcake Cone (Cone, Cake and Frosting): Calories 260 (Calories from Fat 90); Total Fat 11g (Saturated Fat 4.5g); Cholesterol 35mg; Sodium 230mg; Total Carbohydrate 39g (Dietary Fiber 0g)

Frosted Cupcake Cones

Prep Time: 20 min ▪ Start to Finish: 2 hr 35 min ▪ 30 to 36 Cupcake cones

1 box (1 lb 2.25 oz) cake mix with pudding in the mix (any non-swirl flavor)
Water, vegetable oil and eggs called for on cake mix box
30 to 36 flat-bottom ice cream cones
1 container (12 oz) whipped ready-to-spread frosting (any flavor)
Assorted candies and decorations, if desired

1 Heat oven to 350°F. Make cake mix as directed on box, using water, oil and eggs. Fill each cone about half full of batter. Stand cones upright in regular-size muffin cups or 13 × 9-inch pan.

2 Bake 20 to 25 minutes or until toothpick carefully inserted in center comes out clean. Cool completely, about 1 hour.

3 Spread with frosting and decorate. Store loosely covered at room temperature.

1 Cupcake Cone: Calories 170 (Calories from Fat 60); Total Fat 7g (Saturated Fat 1.5g); Cholesterol 20mg; Sodium 135mg; Total Carbohydrate 24g (Dietary Fiber 0g)

Tint the frosting blue for water, and use teddy bear-shaped graham snacks for "people." Add gummy candy rings for inner tubes, gum balls for beach balls and striped gum for inflatable floats.

Surprise Cupcake Cones

Prep Time: 40 min ▮ Start to Finish: 1 hr 25 min ▮ 18 Cupcake cones

1 box (1 lb 2.25 oz) yellow cake mix with pudding in the mix
Water, vegetable oil and eggs called for on cake mix box
18 flat-bottom ice cream cones
1 cup candy-coated chocolate candies
3 containers (12 oz each) strawberry whipped ready-to-spread frosting
1/4 cup multicolored candy sprinkles

1 Heat oven to 350°F. Place paper baking cup in each of 18 regular-size muffin cups; place mini paper baking cup in each of 18 mini muffin cups. Make cake mix as directed on box, using water, oil and eggs. Divide batter evenly among regular and mini muffin cups.

2 Bake mini cupcakes 11 to 13 minutes, regular cupcakes 17 to 22 minutes, or until toothpick inserted in center comes out clean. Remove from pans to cooling rack. Cool completely, about 30 minutes.

3 Tightly cover the tops of 2 empty square or rectangular pans that are at least 2 to 2½ inches deep with heavy-duty foil. Cut 18 "stars" in foil, 3 inches apart, by making slits about 1 inch long with a sharp knife. (This will hold finished cones upright.)

4 Remove paper cups from cupcakes. Place about 2 teaspoons candies in each cone. For each cone, frost top of 1 regular cupcake with frosting; turn upside down onto a cone. Frost bottom (now the top) and side of cupcake. Place mini cupcake upside down on frosted regular cupcake; frost completely (it's easiest to frost from the cone toward the top). Sprinkle with candy sprinkles. Push cone through opening in foil; the foil will keep it upright.

1 Cupcake Cone: Calories 490 (Calories from Fat 190); Total Fat 22g (Saturated Fat 7g); Cholesterol 35mg; Sodium 270mg; Total Carbohydrate 72g (Dietary Fiber 0g)

No strawberry frosting on hand? Tint vanilla frosting a light pink with red food color.

Angel Food Cupcakes

Chocolate Cupcakes

Double-Chocolate Cupcakes

Orange Soda Cupcakes

White Cupcakes

Yellow Cupcakes

Buttercream Frosting

Vanilla Buttercream Frosting

Cream Cheese Frosting

Coconut Cream Frosting

Creamy Chocolate Frosting

Creamy Vanilla Frosting

Creamy White Frosting

White Mountain Frosting

Chocolate Decorator Frosting

White Decorator Frosting

Chocolate Glaze

White Chocolate Glaze

Petits Fours Glaze

Lemon Filling

6

cupcake basics

Angel Food Cupcakes

Prep Time: 20 min ▪ Start to Finish: 1 hr 5 min ▪ 30 Cupcakes

1^1/$_2$ cups powdered sugar

1 cup cake flour

1^1/$_2$ cups egg whites (about 12)

1^1/$_2$ teaspoons cream of tartar

1 cup granulated sugar

1^1/$_2$ teaspoons vanilla

^{1}/$_2$ teaspoon almond extract

^{1}/$_4$ teaspoon salt

1 Move oven rack to lowest position. Heat oven to 375°F. Place paper baking cup in each of 30 regular-size muffin cups. In small bowl, mix powdered sugar and flour; set aside.

2 In large bowl, beat egg whites and cream of tartar with electric mixer on medium speed until foamy. Beat in granulated sugar, 2 tablespoons at a time, on high speed, adding vanilla, almond extract and salt with the last addition of sugar. Continue beating until stiff and glossy. Do not underbeat.

3 Sprinkle sugar-flour mixture, ¼ cup at a time, over meringue, folding in with rubber spatula just until sugar-flour mixture disappears. Divide batter evenly among 30 muffin cups.

4 Bake 15 to 20 minutes or until cracks in cupcakes feel dry and tops spring back when touched lightly. Remove from pan to cooling rack. Cool completely, about 30 minutes.

1 Cupcake: Calories 70 (Calories from Fat 0); Total Fat 0g (Saturated Fat 0g); Cholesterol 0mg; Sodium 40mg; Total Carbohydrate 16g (Dietary Fiber 0g)

Chocolate Angel Food Cupcakes: Substitute ¼ cup unsweetened baking cocoa for ¼ cup of the flour. Omit almond extract.

Chocolate Cupcakes

Prep Time: 15 min ▪ Start to Finish: 1 hr 15 min ▪ 24 Cupcakes

2¼ cups all-purpose flour

1⅔ cups sugar

¾ cup butter or margarine, room temperature

⅔ cup unsweetened baking cocoa

1¼ cups water

1¼ teaspoons baking soda

1 teaspoon salt

¼ teaspoon baking powder

1 teaspoon vanilla

2 eggs

1 Heat oven to 350°F. Place paper baking cup in each of 24 regular-size muffin cups.

2 In large bowl, beat all ingredients with electric mixer on low speed 30 seconds, scraping bowl constantly. Beat on high speed 3 minutes, scraping bowl occasionally. Divide batter evenly among muffin cups.

3 Bake 20 to 25 minutes or until toothpick inserted in center comes out clean. Cool 10 minutes; remove from pan to cooling rack. Cool completely, about 30 minutes.

1 Cupcake: Calories 270 (Calories from Fat 90); Total Fat 10g (Saturated Fat 6g); Cholesterol 65mg; Sodium 240mg; Total Carbohydrate 40g (Dietary Fiber 1g)

Double-Chocolate Cupcakes

Prep Time: 15 min ■ Start to Finish: 1 hr 5 min ■ 24 Cupcakes

2¼ cups all-purpose flour

1¾ cups sugar

½ cup shortening

1½ cups buttermilk

1½ teaspoons baking soda

1 teaspoon salt

1 teaspoon vanilla

2 oz unsweetened baking chocolate, melted and cooled

2 eggs

1 cup miniature chocolate chips

1 Heat oven to 350°F. Grease bottom and sides of 24 regular-size muffin cups with shortening and lightly flour, or line with paper baking cups.

2 In large bowl, beat all ingredients except chocolate chips with electric mixer on medium speed 30 seconds, scraping bowl constantly. Beat on high speed 2 minutes, scraping bowl occasionally. Fold in chocolate chips. Divide batter evenly among muffin cups.

3 Bake 20 to 25 minutes or until toothpick inserted in center comes out clean. Cool 10 minutes; remove from pan to cooling rack. Cool completely, about 30 minutes.

1 Cupcake: Calories 200 (Calories from Fat 70); Total Fat 8g (Saturated Fat 3.5g); Cholesterol 20mg; Sodium 200mg; Total Carbohydrate 29g (Dietary Fiber 1g)

Chocolate-Cherry Cupcakes: Fold in ½ cup chopped maraschino cherries, well drained, with the chocolate chips.

Orange Soda Cupcakes

Prep Time: 15 min ▪ Start to Finish: 1 hr 10 min ▪ 12 Cupcakes

2 cups all-purpose flour
³/₄ cup sugar
¹/₃ cup butter or margarine, softened
1 cup orange-flavored soda pop
1 teaspoon baking powder
¹/₂ teaspoon baking soda
¹/₂ teaspoon salt
¹/₂ teaspoon finely shredded orange peel
2 eggs

1 Heat oven to 350°F. Place paper baking cups in each of 12. Grease bottom and sides of 12 regular-size muffin cups.

2 In medium bowl, beat all ingredients with electric mixer on low speed 30 seconds, scraping bowl occasionally. Beat on medium speed 2 minutes, scraping bowl occasionally. Divide batter evenly among muffin cups.

3 Bake 20 to 25 minutes or until toothpick inserted in center comes out clean. Cool completely, about 30 minutes.

1 Cupcake: Calories 190 (Calories from Fat 60); Total Fat 6g (Saturated Fat 3.5g); Cholesterol 50mg; Sodium 240mg; Total Carbohydrate 31g (Dietary Fiber 0g)

White Cupcakes

Prep Time: 15 min ▪ Start to Finish: 1 hr 15 min ▪ 24 Cupcakes

2¹/₄ cups all-purpose flour	3¹/₂ teaspoons baking powder
1²/₃ cups sugar	1 teaspoon salt
²/₃ cup shortening	1 teaspoon vanilla
1¹/₄ cups milk	5 egg whites

1 Heat oven to 350°F. Grease bottom and sides of 24 regular-size or 36 mini muffin cups with shortening and lightly flour, or line with paper baking cups.

2 In large bowl, beat all ingredients except egg whites with electric mixer on low speed 30 seconds, scraping bowl constantly. Beat on high speed 2 minutes, scraping bowl occasionally. Beat in egg whites on high speed 2 minutes, scraping bowl occasionally. Divide batter evenly among muffin cups.

3 Bake 20 to 25 minutes for regular-size muffin cups or 10 to 15 minutes for mini muffin cups, or until toothpick inserted in center comes out clean or until cake springs back when touched lightly in center. Cool 10 minutes; remove from pan to cooling rack. Cool completely, about 1 hour.

1 Cupcake: Calories 150 (Calories from Fat 45); Total Fat 5g (Saturated Fat 1.5g); Cholesterol 0mg; Sodium 170mg; Total Carbohydrate 25g (Dietary Fiber 0g)

Almond Cupcakes: Substitute 1 teaspoon almond extract for the vanilla.

Hazelnut Cupcakes: Add 1 cup ground hazelnuts (filberts) with ingredients.

Marble Cupcakes: Pour half of batter into another bowl. Mix 2 ounces unsweetened baking chocolate, melted and cooled, 1 tablespoon sugar, 2 tablespoons warm water and ¼ teaspoon baking soda. Stir into one batter. Spoon light and dark batters alternately into muffin cups. Cut through batter once or twice for marbled design.

Pastel Marble Cupcakes: Divide batter into 3 equal parts. Tint one part with 2 or 3 drops red food color and one part with 2 or 3 drops green food color; leave other part plain. Spoon batters alternately into muffin cups. Cut through batter once or twice for marbled design.

Yellow Cupcakes

Prep Time: 15 min   Start to Finish: 1 hr 15 min   24 Cupcakes

2$1/4$ cups all-purpose flour
1$1/4$ cups sugar
$1/2$ cup butter or margarine, softened
1$1/4$ cups milk
3 teaspoons baking powder
1 teaspoon salt
1 teaspoon vanilla
3 large eggs

1 Heat oven to 350°F. Place paper baking cup in each of 24 regular-size muffin cups.

2 In large bowl, beat all ingredients with electric mixer on low speed 30 seconds, scraping bowl constantly. Beat on high speed 3 minutes, scraping bowl occasionally. Divide batter evenly among muffin cups.

3 Bake 20 to 25 minutes until toothpick inserted in center comes out clean. Cool 10 minutes; remove from pan to cooling rack. Cool completely, about 30 minutes.

1 Cupcake: Calories 220 (Calories from Fat 70); Total Fat 8g (Saturated Fat 4.5g); Cholesterol 45mg; Sodium 220mg; Total Carbohydrate 30g (Dietary Fiber 0g)

Orange-Coconut Cupcakes: Omit vanilla. Add 1 tablespoon grated orange peel and 1 cup flaked coconut with ingredients.

Lemon–Poppy Seed Cupcakes: Omit vanilla. Add 1 tablespoon grated lemon peel and 2 tablespoons poppy seed with ingredients.

Buttercream Frosting

Prep Time: 10 min ▪ Start to Finish: 10 min ▪ 3 cups

4 cups powdered sugar
$1/2$ cup butter or margarine, softened
$1/2$ cup shortening
2 to 3 tablespoons milk
1 teaspoon vanilla or almond extract

In large bowl, beat powdered sugar, butter and shortening with electric mixer on low speed until blended. Beat in milk and vanilla on medium speed until smooth. If necessary, stir in milk, a few drops at a time, until spreadable.

2 Tablespoons: Calories 150 (Calories from Fat 70); Total Fat 8g (Saturated Fat 3g); Cholesterol 10mg; Sodium 25mg; Total Carbohydrate 20g (Dietary Fiber 0g)

Vanilla Buttercream Frosting

Prep Time: 10 min ▪ Start to Finish: 10 min ▪ 12 Servings (about $1^3/_4$ cups)

3 cups powdered sugar
$1/3$ cup butter or margarine, room temperature
$1^1/_2$ teaspoons vanilla
1 to 2 tablespoons milk

In a medium bowl, mix the powdered sugar and butter with a spoon or electric mixer on low speed until well mixed. Stir in vanilla and 1 tablespoon of the milk. Gradually beat in just enough remaining milk to make frosting smooth and spreadable. If frosting is too thick, beat in more milk, a few drops at a time. If frosting becomes too thin, beat in a small amount of powdered sugar.

1 Serving: Calories 165 (Calories from Fat 45); Total Fat 5g (Saturated Fat 3g); Cholesterol 15mg; Sodium 35mg; Total Carbohydrate 30g (Dietary Fiber 0g)

Peanut Butter Buttercream Frosting: Substitute peanut butter for the butter. Increase milk to ¼ cup, adding more if necessary, a few drops at a time.

Cream Cheese Frosting

Prep Time: 10 min ▪ Start to Finish: 10 min ▪ About 2½ cups

 1 package (8 oz) cream cheese, softened
 1 tablespoon milk
 1 teaspoon vanilla
 4 cups powdered sugar

In large bowl, beat cream cheese, milk and vanilla with electric mixer on low speed until smooth. Gradually beat in powdered sugar, 1 cup at a time, until smooth and spreadable. Refrigerate any remaining frosted cupcakes.

2 Tablespoons: Calories 140 (Calories from Fat 35); Total Fat 4g (Saturated Fat 2.5g); Cholesterol 15mg; Sodium 35mg; Total Carbohydrate 24g (Dietary Fiber 0g)

Coconut Cream Frosting

Prep Time: 10 min ▪ Start to Finish: 10 min ▪ About 3 cups

 3 cups powdered sugar
 1/3 cup butter or margarine, softened
 1/4 teaspoon salt
 1 teaspoon coconut extract
 1 to 3 tablespoons milk

In medium bowl, beat powdered sugar, butter and salt with spoon or with electric mixer until well blended. Beat in coconut extract and 1 tablespoon milk. Gradually beat in just enough remaining milk to make frosting smooth and spreadable.

2 Tablespoons: Calories 80 (Calories from Fat 25); Total Fat 2.5g (Saturated Fat 1.5g); Cholesterol 5mg; Sodium 40mg; Total Carbohydrate 15g (Dietary Fiber 0g)

Creamy Chocolate Frosting

Prep Time: 5 min ▪ Start to Finish: 5 min ▪ 2 ¼ cups

½ cup butter or margarine, softened	3 cups powdered sugar
3 oz unsweetened baking chocolate, melted and cooled	2 teaspoons vanilla
	About 3 tablespoons milk

In large bowl, mix butter and chocolate with spoon or electric mixer on low speed. Beat in powdered sugar. Beat in vanilla and milk until smooth and spreadable.

2 Tablespoons: Calories 160 (Calories from Fat 70); Total Fat 8g (Saturated Fat 4g); Cholesterol 15mg; Sodium 35mg; Total Carbohydrate 21g (Dietary Fiber 0g)

Creamy Cocoa Frosting: Substitute ½ cup unsweetened baking cocoa for the chocolate.

Creamy Vanilla Frosting

Prep Time: 5 min ▪ Start to Finish: 5 min ▪ About 4 cups

5 ½ cups powdered sugar	2 teaspoons vanilla
⅔ cup butter or margarine, softened	About 3 tablespoons milk

In large bowl, beat powdered sugar and butter with spoon or electric mixer on low speed. Beat in vanilla and milk until smooth and spreadable.

2 Tablespoons: Calories 160 (Calories from Fat 45); Total Fat 5g (Saturated Fat 2.5g); Cholesterol 15mg; Sodium 35mg; Total Carbohydrate 28g (Dietary Fiber 0g)

Creamy Almond Frosting: Substitute 1½ teaspoons almond extract for the vanilla.

Creamy Citrus Frosting: Omit vanilla. Substitute lemon or orange juice for the milk. Stir in ½ teaspoon grated lemon peel or 2 teaspoons grated orange peel.

Peanut Butter Frosting: Substitute peanut butter for the butter. Increase milk to ¼ to ⅓ cup.

Creamy White Frosting

Prep Time: 5 min ▮ Start to Finish: 5 min ▮ About 3 cups

4 cups powdered sugar
$\frac{1}{2}$ cup shortening
$\frac{1}{2}$ teaspoon clear vanilla or almond extract
2 to 3 tablespoons milk

In large bowl, beat powdered sugar and shortening with spoon or electric mixer on low speed. Beat in vanilla and milk until smooth and spreadable.

2 Tablespoons: Calories 120 (Calories from Fat 40); Total Fat 4.5g (Saturated Fat 1g); Cholesterol 0mg; Sodium 0mg; Total Carbohydrate 20g (Dietary Fiber 0g)

White Mountain Frosting

Prep Time: 25 min   Start to Finish: 35 min   3 cups

2 egg whites
$\frac{1}{2}$ cup sugar
$\frac{1}{4}$ cup light corn syrup
2 tablespoons water
1 teaspoon vanilla

1 In medium bowl, beat egg whites with electric mixer on high speed just until stiff peaks form; set aside.

2 In 1-quart saucepan, stir sugar, corn syrup and water until well mixed. Cover and heat to rolling boil over medium heat. Uncover and boil 4 to 8 minutes, without stirring, to 242°F on candy thermometer or until small amount of mixture dropped into cup of very cold water forms a firm ball that holds its shape until pressed. For an accurate temperature reading, tilt the saucepan slightly so mixture is deep enough for thermometer.

3 Pour hot syrup very slowly in thin stream into egg whites, beating constantly on medium speed. Add vanilla. Beat on high speed about 10 minutes or until stiff peaks form.

2 Tablespoons: Calories 30 (Calories from Fat 0); Total Fat 0g (Saturated Fat 0g); Cholesterol 0mg; Sodium 10mg; Total Carbohydrate 7g (Dietary Fiber 0g)

Fluffy Brown Sugar Frosting: Substitute packed brown sugar for the granulated sugar and decrease vanilla to ½ teaspoon.

Fluffy Cocoa Frosting: Sift ¼ cup unsweetened baking cocoa over frosting and fold in until blended.

Chocolate Decorator Frosting

Prep Time: 10 min ▮ Start to Finish: 10 min ▮ About 1 cup

1 oz unsweetened baking chocolate, chopped
1 teaspoon butter or margarine
1 cup powdered sugar
1 to 2 tablespoons boiling water

In 1-quart saucepan, melt chocolate and butter over low heat, stirring occasionally; remove from heat. Stir in powdered sugar and 1 tablespoon water. Beat with spoon until smooth. Beat in additional water, 1 teaspoon at a time, until spreadable.

2 Tablespoons: Calories 90 (Calories from Fat 20); Total Fat 2.5g (Saturated Fat 1.5g); Cholesterol 0mg; Sodium 0mg; Total Carbohydrate 16g (Dietary Fiber 0g)

White Decorator Frosting

Prep Time: 10 min ▮ Start to Finish: 10 min ▮ About 4 cups

6$^1/_4$ cups powdered sugar
$^3/_4$ cup shortening
$^3/_4$ teaspoon vanilla or almond extract
$^1/_2$ cup milk

In large bowl, beat powdered sugar and shortening with spoon or electric mixer on low speed until smooth. Beat in vanilla and milk until smooth. If necessary, stir in additional milk, a few drops at a time, until smooth and spreadable.

2 Tablespoons: Calories 140 (Calories from Fat 45); Total Fat 5g (Saturated Fat 1g); Cholesterol 0mg; Sodium 0mg; Total Carbohydrate 24g (Dietary Fiber 0g)

Chocolate Glaze

Prep Time: 10 min ▪ Start to Finish: 20 min ▪ About 1 cup

1 bag (6 oz) semisweet chocolate chips (1 cup)
$^1/_4$ cup butter or margarine
2 tablespoons light corn syrup

In 1-quart saucepan, heat all ingredients over low heat, stirring constantly, until chocolate chips are melted and mixture is smooth and thin enough to drizzle. Cool slightly.

1 Tablespoon: Calories 90 (Calories from Fat 50); Total Fat 6g (Saturated Fat 3.5g); Cholesterol 10mg; Sodium 25mg; Total Carbohydrate 9g (Dietary Fiber 0g)

White Chocolate Glaze

Prep Time: 10 min ▪ Start to Finish: 10 min ▪ About $^1/_2$ cup

$^1/_2$ cup white vanilla baking chips
2 tablespoons light corn syrup
$1^1/_2$ teaspoons water

In 1-quart saucepan, heat all ingredients over low heat, stirring constantly, until chips are melted and mixture is smooth and thin enough to drizzle. Cool slightly.

1 Tablespoon: Calories 110 (Calories from Fat 50); Total Fat 5g (Saturated Fat 3g); Cholesterol 0mg; Sodium 20mg; Total Carbohydrate 14g (Dietary Fiber 0g)

Petits Fours Glaze

Prep Time: 10 min   Start to Finish: 10 min   About 3 cups

1 bag (2 lb) powdered sugar	2 teaspoons almond extract
¹/₂ cup water	1 to 3 teaspoons hot water
¹/₂ cup light corn syrup	

In 3-quart saucepan, stir all ingredients except hot water. Heat over low heat, stirring frequently, until sugar is dissolved; remove from heat. Stir in hot water, 1 teaspoon at a time, until glaze is pourable.

1 Tablespoon: Calories 90 (Calories from Fat 0); Total Fat 0g (Saturated Fat 0g); Cholesterol 0mg; Sodium 0mg; Total Carbohydrate 21g (Dietary Fiber 0g)

Lemon Filling

Prep Time: 5 min   Start to Finish: 2 hr 15 min   12 servings

³/₄ cup sugar	1 tablespoon butter or margarine
3 tablespoons cornstarch	1 teaspoon grated lemon peel
¹/₄ teaspoon salt	¹/₄ cup lemon juice
²/₃ cup water	2 drops yellow food color, if desired

1 Mix sugar, cornstarch and salt in 1½-quart saucepan. Gradually stir in water. Cook over medium heat, stirring constantly, until mixture thickens and boils. Boil and stir 1 minute; remove from heat.

2 Stir in butter and lemon peel until butter is melted. Gradually stir in lemon juice and food color. Press plastic wrap on filling to prevent a tough layer from forming on top. Refrigerate about 2 hours or until set. Store cupcakes filled with Lemon Filling covered in the refrigerator.

1 Serving: Calories 70 (Calories from Fat 10); Total Fat 1g (Saturated Fat 1g); Cholesterol 5mg; Sodium 55mg; Total Carbohydrate 15g (Dietary Fiber 0g)

Helpful Nutrition and Cooking Information

Recommended intake for a daily diet of 2,000 calories as set by the Food and Drug Administration

Total Fat	Less than 65g
Saturated Fat	Less than 20g
Cholesterol	Less than 300mg
Sodium	Less than 2,400mg
Total Carbohydrate	300g
Dietary Fiber	25g

Calculating Nutrition Information

- The first ingredient was used wherever a choice is given (such as ⅓ cup sour cream or plain yogurt).

- The first ingredient amount was used wherever a range is given (such as 2 to 3 teaspoons).

- The first serving number was used wherever a range is given (such as 4 to 6 servings).

- "If desired" ingredients and recipe variations were not included (such as sprinkle with brown sugar, if desired).

- Only the amount of a marinade or frying oil that is absorbed by the food during preparation was calculated.

Ingredients Used in Recipe Testing and Nutrition Calculations

- The following ingredients, based on most commonly purchased ingredients, were used unless otherwise indicated: large eggs, 2% milk, 80%-lean ground beef, canned chicken broth and vegetable oil spread containing at least 65% fat when margarine is used.

- Solid vegetable shortening (not butter, margarine, or nonstick cooking spray) was used to grease pans unless otherwise indicated.

Equipment Used in Recipe Testing

- Cookware and bakeware without nonstick coatings were used, unless otherwise indicated.

- No dark-colored, black or insulated bakeware was used.

- When a pan is specified, a metal pan was used; a baking dish or pie plate means ovenproof glass was used.

- An electric hand mixer was used for mixing when mixer speeds are specified.

Metric Conversion Guide

VOLUME

U.S. Units	Canadian Metric	Australian Metric
1/4 teaspoon	1 mL	1 ml
1/2 teaspoon	2 mL	2 ml
1 teaspoon	5 mL	5 ml
1 tablespoon	15 mL	20 ml
1/4 cup	50 mL	60 ml
1/3 cup	75 mL	80 ml
1/2 cup	125 mL	125 ml
2/3 cup	150 mL	170 ml
3/4 cup	175 mL	190 ml
1 cup	250 mL	250 ml
1 quart	1 liter	1 liter
1 1/2 quarts	1.5 liters	1.5 liters
2 quarts	2 liters	2 liters
2 1/2 quarts	2.5 liters	2.5 liters
3 quarts	3 liters	3 liters
4 quarts	4 liters	4 liters

WEIGHT

U.S. Units	Canadian Metric	Australian Metric
1 ounce	30 grams	30 grams
2 ounces	55 grams	60 grams
3 ounces	85 grams	90 grams
4 ounces (1/4 pound)	115 grams	125 grams
8 ounces (1/2 pound)	225 grams	225 grams
16 ounces (1 pound)	455 grams	500 grams
1 pound	455 grams	1/2 kilogram

MEASUREMENTS

Inches	Centimeters
1	2.5
2	5.0
3	7.5
4	10.0
5	12.5
6	15.0
7	17.5
8	20.5
9	23.0
10	25.5
11	28.0
12	30.5
13	33.0

TEMPERATURES

Fahrenheit	Celsius
32°	0°
212°	100°
250°	120°
275°	140°
300°	150°
325°	160°
350°	180°
375°	190°
400°	200°
425°	220°
450°	230°
475°	240°
500°	260°

NOTE: The recipes in this cookbook have not been developed or tested using metric measures. When converting recipes to metric, some variations in quality may be noted.

Index

Page numbers in italics indicate illustrations.

Whatever's on the menu, make it easy with *Betty Crocker*